The Ultimate Living Trust & Estate Planning Blueprint

The Complete Easy-to-Follow Guide to Protecting Your Assets, Safeguarding Your Family's Future, and Creating a Lasting Legacy

Ernest Garrett

Introduction

Most people do not delay estate planning because they are careless. They delay because the subject feels heavy. It forces them to think about illness, death, money, family tension, and legal systems they do not fully understand. Even people who are responsible in every other part of life can put this off for years. They tell themselves they will handle it after the next move, after retirement, after the kids settle down, after business gets less busy, or after they find the right lawyer. Time passes. Life changes. Assets grow. Responsibilities grow. The plan stays unfinished.

That delay is understandable, but it comes with a price. When no clear plan exists, the law steps in with default rules. Those rules may not reflect what you want, how your family works, or what your property needs. Estate planning exists to prevent that gap between your wishes and what actually happens. The American Bar Association describes estate planning as a process that looks at your goals, your assets, how they are owned, and your family structure. It covers transfer at death, but it also covers other personal matters and may include tools such as wills, revocable trusts, powers of attorney, and health care directives.

That is the first idea this book wants to make clear. Estate planning is not a stack of papers. It is a system for protecting people. Your property matters, of course. Your house matters. Your savings matter. Your business matters. But the deeper purpose is to protect the people who will be left to handle things when you cannot. A good plan gives instructions. It names decision-makers. It reduces room for guesswork. It cuts down on confusion at the worst possible time.

This is also why estate planning is not only for the wealthy. Trusts are often treated like luxury planning tools, as if they belong only to people with large estates, complicated investments, or multiple properties. That is not true. The ABA notes that trusts are not only for wealthy families and that even young parents with limited assets may use them to protect children and manage property responsibly. The question is not whether you are rich enough to plan. The real question is whether the people you care about would benefit from a clearer path if something happened to you.

Once you see estate planning in that light, the subject becomes easier to understand. It is about three things. First, who gets what. Second, who handles what. Third, how smoothly the transition happens. A weak plan leaves those questions open. A strong plan answers them before there is pressure, grief, or conflict. This book is built to help you answer them in plain language and in a practical order.

One of the biggest reasons people turn to living trusts is probate. Probate sounds mysterious when you first hear it, but the core idea is simple. Probate is the legal process used to transfer or inherit property after the owner has died. If court involvement is required, that is what people usually mean when they say an estate is "going through probate." California Courts explains that an estate may need probate even if the person had a will, because the court still may need to appoint a personal representative, gather property, pay bills, and distribute what remains.

That point matters more than many people realize. A will is important, but a will by itself does not avoid probate. In fact, a will is often the document that tells the probate court what should happen. So when families think, "We have a will, so everything is handled," they may be surprised by the amount of work that still follows. Court filings may be needed. Deadlines may apply. Financial institutions may require proof of authority. Property may need to be collected, valued, protected, and distributed. Debts and taxes may need attention before heirs receive anything.

This is where a living trust enters the picture. A living trust is a trust created during your lifetime. It is often revocable, which means you can amend it or cancel it while you are alive and competent. You can usually serve as your own trustee while you are living, which means you keep practical control over your own property. The trust becomes powerful not because it takes control away from you, but because it creates a legal structure that can continue to operate if you become ill, disabled, or die. The ABA explains that a living trust can help manage your assets during life, protect you if you become ill or disabled, and direct property after death.

That continuity is one of the strongest reasons people use a living trust. If you become unable to act, a successor trustee you have already named can step in according to the terms of the trust. If you die, that same structure continues, and the trustee follows the instructions you left behind. In a properly built and funded trust, the property in the trust does not have to pass through probate in the same way property held in your individual name does. The trust already owns the property, and the trustee already has authority under the trust instrument to manage and distribute it according to the trust terms.

But this is also the place where many guides oversell. A living trust is useful, but it is not magic. It does not fix property that was never transferred to the trust. It does not replace every other planning document. It does not automatically erase taxes, fees, delays, or family disputes. The ABA states clearly that a living trust can almost never totally avoid probate and that a simple pour-over will is usually still needed to move into the trust any probate property that was not transferred during life. A court self-help resource from Santa Clara County also notes that if the settlor intended property to be in the trust but died without changing title, the trustee may need to petition the court to include the property as part of the trust.

This is why funding matters so much. Funding a trust means changing ownership of selected assets so that the trust, not you as an individual, holds legal title. If a trust is signed and then placed in a drawer while the house deed, financial accounts, and other intended assets stay outside it, the trust may look complete but fail in the exact moment it is supposed to help. A trust works best when its instructions and its ownership structure match. This book will return to that point often because it is one of the most common places where good intentions break down.

Another reason many people choose a living trust is privacy. A will admitted to probate is generally part of a court process, and the ABA notes that a will is technically a matter of public record. A living trust, by contrast, is often kept private and in many states does not need to be filed with a court to be effective. That privacy can matter to families who do not want details of relationships, distributions, or personal decisions exposed through a public process. At the same time, privacy should be understood honestly. It is a benefit, not a promise that no information will ever become public under any circumstance.

Taxes are another area full of confusion. Many people hear the word "trust" and assume tax savings automatically follow. That is one of the oldest misunderstandings in estate planning. The ABA explains that revocable living trusts are often incorrectly presented as uniquely favorable for tax purposes.

The IRS and ABA both explain that because the grantor retains the power to revoke the trust, the assets in a revocable trust are generally treated as still belonging to the grantor for income and estate tax purposes. In plain language, a standard revocable living trust is usually a management and transfer tool, not a special tax shelter.

That does not mean taxes never matter in estate planning. They do. It means tax planning has to be done with the right tools and the right expectations. For many readers, the bigger problem is not federal estate tax. The bigger problem is disorder. Bills that cannot be paid quickly. Accounts that get frozen. Property that no one has clear authority to manage. Family members who are forced to chase institutions for documents while also grieving. Trust planning helps most when it solves those real-life problems with clarity and structure.

It is also important to understand that estate planning is not only about death. Many families face a more difficult situation first: incapacity. Someone is still alive, but memory is slipping. A stroke happens. A serious accident changes everything. A parent can no longer manage bills, sign documents, or understand complex decisions. If no one has legal authority to step in, the family may be pushed toward court involvement at the exact time they have the least energy for it.

This is why a complete plan almost always includes a power of attorney and health care instructions alongside any trust. The Consumer Financial Protection Bureau explains that a power of attorney allows someone else to act on your behalf and can help you plan ahead by naming a trusted person to act if you cannot. The CFPB also warns that without a power of attorney, a family member may have to go to court to have a guardian appointed, which can be lengthy, expensive, and public. The ABA adds that a power of attorney is accepted in all states, though the rules differ from state to state, and that it lets you choose who will act for you and define the limits of that authority.

Health care planning belongs beside financial planning for the same reason. The ABA explains that a living will or advance health care directive is your written expression of how you want to be treated in certain medical circumstances, including choices about life-sustaining treatment and other end-of-life decisions. If your financial plan is clear but your medical wishes are not, your family may still face painful uncertainty. A complete plan respects both money and dignity.

You will notice that this book keeps returning to one theme: clarity prevents damage. Clear language prevents misreading. Clear authority prevents delay. Clear beneficiary choices prevent conflict. Clear funding prevents failure. Clear instructions reduce the chance that your family will have to guess what you wanted. This does not mean a good estate plan removes all emotion or all work. It means the plan removes avoidable confusion so your family can spend less time untangling and more time healing.

That is also why this guide is built in plain English. Estate planning can become hard to follow not because the ideas are impossible, but because they are often explained badly. Readers are buried under undefined terms, long explanations, and abstract legal theory before they understand the basic structure. This book takes the opposite route. It starts with what matters most, explains terms only when needed, and connects each step to the reason behind it. You should know not only what to do, but why it matters and what can go wrong if it is ignored.

As you move through these pages, you will see that a living trust is best understood as part of a complete plan, not as a stand-alone cure. You may still need a will. You may need powers of attorney. You may need health care directives. You may need to review title on your home, check beneficiary designations on retirement accounts and insurance, and think through who should act for you if you cannot act for yourself. The ABA notes that title and beneficiary designations can control what happens to many assets, sometimes regardless of what a will says. So a sound plan is not just about drafting documents. It is about making the documents and the ownership structure work together.

This is where many people feel overwhelmed. They assume a good plan must be complicated because life is complicated. But the truth is different. A good plan must be clear enough to work under stress. It should reflect your real life, not an imaginary perfect one. It should fit your family, your property, your values, and your level of complexity. It should be thorough, but not bloated. Simple where simple is enough. Detailed where detail protects the people you love.

If that sounds doable, that is because it is. You do not need to become a lawyer to understand the framework. You do not need to memorize every rule before you begin. You do need to stop treating the subject like a distant task for another season of life. The sooner you understand the logic of living trusts and estate planning, the sooner you can replace uncertainty with structure.

That is what this blueprint is for. It is here to help you think clearly, choose wisely, and act in the right order. It will show you what probate is and why people want to reduce it. It will show you what a living trust can do, what it cannot do, and where people get misled. It will show you how to protect assets without losing sight of the people those assets are meant to serve. It will show you how to prepare for incapacity, not just death. It will show you how to reduce the odds of conflict, delay, and administrative confusion. Most of all, it will help you create a plan that works in real life, when emotions are high and the margin for error is low.

You worked for what you have. Maybe it is a modest estate. Maybe it is substantial. Either way, it carries the story of your effort. Your plan should honor that effort. It should not leave your family with locked assets, scattered instructions, unclear authority, and painful guesswork. It should give them direction. It should give them legal footing. It should give them peace where peace is possible.

That is the promise of good estate planning. Not perfection. Not control over every future event. But a far better chance that your wishes will be known, your property will be managed with care, and your loved ones will not be left to sort through unnecessary disorder on their own.

Chapter 1: The Foundation of Estate Planning

What Is Estate Planning?

Estate planning is the process of preparing for the future by organizing the management and distribution of your assets in the event of your incapacity or death. It is more than just writing a will or deciding who gets what after you pass away. Estate planning involves making decisions about how your property, money, and personal affairs will be handled while you're alive, if you're incapacitated, and after you pass on.

At its core, estate planning ensures that your assets are distributed according to your wishes, your loved ones are taken care of, and your family's future is secure. It includes a variety of documents that can be set in place to protect your assets and direct their use in the way you want, even after you are no longer able to manage things yourself.

Estate planning doesn't just focus on the distribution of money or property. It also addresses who will make decisions for you in case you become incapacitated, who will be in charge of your health care decisions, and how any businesses or valuable assets will be passed on or managed.

A major part of estate planning is choosing the right tools and ensuring they fit your goals and needs. Tools such as living trusts, wills, powers of attorney, and health care directives all work together to form a comprehensive plan that addresses your health, finances, and legacy. The ultimate goal is to reduce the risk of family disputes, minimize taxes, and avoid the lengthy and expensive process of probate.

Why Estate Planning Is Essential for Everyone

Many people mistakenly think that estate planning is only necessary for the wealthy or elderly. This couldn't be further from the truth. Estate planning is essential for everyone, regardless of age or financial situation. In fact, the sooner you start planning, the better it is for you and your loved ones.

The purpose of estate planning is not just about planning for death—it's about planning for life. Having an estate plan in place helps you retain control over how your assets are managed, how decisions are made on your behalf, and how your family is provided for, especially if you are no longer able to handle things yourself. Without a plan, your family may face significant difficulties, such as long delays in settling your affairs, legal battles, and confusion about who is responsible for what.

Additionally, an estate plan protects your family from being exposed to unnecessary taxes and fees that can be a result of poor planning. A good estate plan minimizes the financial burden on your heirs and can help prevent family conflicts, which can be very common in the absence of clear guidance.

Incapacity planning is also a significant aspect of estate planning. For example, if you become mentally or physically incapable of managing your affairs, estate planning documents like a power of attorney can designate someone you trust to take care of your financial and medical matters. Without such documents in place, your loved ones could face difficulties in obtaining the legal authority to manage your affairs, potentially leading to time-consuming and expensive court processes.

The Difference Between a Will and a Living Trust

While both a will and a living trust are key components of estate planning, they serve different purposes and have different benefits. It's essential to understand the distinction between the two to ensure you choose the best tools for your needs.

A Will

A will is a legal document that expresses your wishes regarding the distribution of your assets after you pass away. It also allows you to designate guardians for your minor children. A will must go through probate, which is a court-supervised process of validating the will, paying any debts, and distributing your assets according to the terms of the will. This can be a lengthy and expensive process, and probate records are public, meaning the details of your estate can be accessed by anyone.

One of the main advantages of a will is its simplicity and ease of creation. It's a straightforward way to ensure that your wishes are known and carried out after your death. However, since it must go through probate, it often results in delays and expenses for your family.

A Living Trust

A living trust, on the other hand, is a legal document that allows you to transfer ownership of your assets to a trust during your lifetime. The trust is managed by a trustee (you, or someone you designate) while you are alive, and after your death, the trustee will distribute the assets to your beneficiaries according to your instructions. One of the main advantages of a living trust is that it avoids probate. This means that your assets can be distributed without going through the lengthy, public court process.

A living trust can also help if you become incapacitated. Since you have designated a successor trustee, the trust can continue to operate without court intervention, allowing your assets to be managed by someone you trust until you are able to take control again, if ever. Additionally, because a living trust is not subject to probate, it is a private matter, and the details of your estate are not made public.

However, one of the main challenges of a living trust is ensuring it is properly funded. To work, a living trust must own the property that you wish to pass through it. If assets are not properly transferred to the trust, they may still need to go through probate.

Key Terminology You Need to Know

To understand estate planning fully, it's important to be familiar with key terminology. These terms will appear throughout your estate planning process and in the documents you create. Here are some of the most common terms:

- **Beneficiary**: A person or entity who is designated to receive assets or benefits from your estate or trust. Beneficiaries can include family members, charities, or even pets (if specified in a trust).
- **Trustee**: The person or institution responsible for managing and distributing the assets in a trust. The trustee is legally bound to follow the instructions of the trust and act in the best interests of the beneficiaries.
- **Grantor**: The person who creates and funds the trust. In the case of a living trust, the grantor is the person who sets up the trust and transfers assets into it.
- **Power of Attorney (POA)**: A legal document that gives someone the authority to make decisions on your behalf, either for financial or medical matters, when you are unable to act for yourself.
- **Health Care Directive**: A document that outlines your preferences regarding medical treatment in the event you are unable to communicate your wishes. This can include decisions about life support, organ donation, and end-of-life care.
- **Estate**: The total value of all assets (property, bank accounts, investments, etc.) that a person owns at the time of their death.
- **Probate**: The legal process of validating a will and administering an estate. This process can be time-consuming and costly, which is why many people seek to avoid it through tools like living trusts.
- **Guardian**: A person who is legally appointed to care for minor children in the event of the parents' death or incapacity.

Common Estate Planning Mistakes to Avoid

Estate planning can be complicated, and many people make mistakes along the way. Some of the most common errors include:

1. **Failing to Create an Estate Plan**

   Many people procrastinate on estate planning or assume it's not necessary until later in life. However, unexpected events can happen at any age, and an estate plan ensures that your wishes are known and carried out if the unexpected occurs.

1. **Not Updating Your Plan Regularly**

   Life changes, and so should your estate plan. Major life events such as marriage, divorce, the birth of children, or the purchase of a new property should trigger a review of your estate plan. Failing to update your plan means your wishes may no longer align with your current situation.

1. **Not Funding Your Living Trust**

   A living trust is only effective if it is funded properly. Many people make the mistake of signing a trust but failing to transfer ownership of their assets into it. If assets are not titled in the name of the trust, they may still need to go through probate.

1. **Not Communicating with Family Members**

   It's important to keep your family informed about your estate plan. Failing to do so can lead to confusion and disputes after your death. Clearly communicate your wishes and make sure your family knows where your important documents are stored.

1. **Choosing the Wrong Executor or Trustee**

Choosing someone who is not qualified or willing to carry out your estate plan can cause problems down the road. Be sure to choose someone who is responsible, trustworthy, and capable of handling the duties required.

1. **Underestimating the Importance of Incapacity Planning**

Many people focus on what happens after their death but neglect to plan for incapacity. Without a durable power of attorney or health care directive, your family may need to go to court to gain the authority to act on your behalf if you are unable to manage your affairs.

1. **Ignoring Tax Implications**

Estate planning isn't just about passing on assets—it's also about minimizing taxes. Failure to understand how estate taxes work and how to plan for them can result in your beneficiaries facing unnecessary financial burdens.

1. **Relying Too Heavily on DIY Tools**

While DIY estate planning tools can be tempting, they can often lead to mistakes or omissions. It's important to consult with an estate planning attorney, especially if you have a complex estate or unique family dynamics.

By avoiding these common mistakes, you can ensure that your estate plan is thorough, effective, and capable of achieving your goals.

Chapter 2: Understanding Probate and How to Avoid It

What Is Probate?

Probate is the legal process that is required after someone passes away in order to validate their will and distribute their assets. If there is no will, the process is still required to determine who will inherit the decedent's property according to state laws. The court oversees this process, ensuring that debts and taxes are paid before any remaining assets are distributed to heirs or beneficiaries.

In simple terms, probate is the court's way of overseeing the transition of property from one person to another after death. It ensures that the deceased's affairs are in order, debts are paid, and assets are distributed according to either the decedent's will or state law.

Key Steps in the Probate Process:

1. **Filing the Will**: The first step in probate is to file the deceased person's will with the probate court. If there is no will, the court follows the state's intestacy laws to decide how to distribute the assets.
2. **Appointment of Executor/Administrator**: The court will appoint someone to administer the estate. If a will exists, the named executor is appointed. If no will exists, the court appoints an administrator.
3. **Inventory of Assets**: The executor or administrator will identify and take inventory of the decedent's assets. This includes real property, financial accounts, personal belongings, etc.
4. **Paying Debts and Taxes**: The executor is responsible for paying any outstanding debts and taxes owed by the decedent from the estate's funds.
5. **Distribution of Assets**: Once debts and taxes are settled, the remaining assets are distributed to the beneficiaries or heirs as per the will or state law.

Probate can be a relatively simple process if the estate is small and uncomplicated. However, it can become lengthy and complex when there are multiple assets, debts, or potential disputes among family members. In some cases, the probate process can take months or even years to complete.

How Probate Costs Families Time and Money

One of the most significant disadvantages of probate is the cost and time it can take. It is a court-supervised process, meaning that the estate must go through legal proceedings that are not only costly but also time-consuming.

1. Financial Costs of Probate

Probate involves several fees, which can add up quickly. Here are some of the costs families may encounter:

- **Court Fees**: Probate court fees can be significant, as the estate is required to go through the court system. The fees depend on the complexity of the estate and the state in which probate is filed.
- **Executor/Administrator Fees**: The person appointed as the executor or administrator of the estate is entitled to compensation. This fee can vary based on the size of the estate and the state's laws but can range from 1% to 5% of the estate's value.
- **Attorney Fees**: Often, the executor will hire an attorney to navigate the probate process. Attorneys charge hourly rates, and their fees can add up quickly, particularly for complex estates.
- **Appraisal Fees**: In order to determine the value of the estate's assets, appraisers may need to be hired, especially if there are unique or valuable assets such as art, real estate, or collectibles.
- **Bond Fees**: If the estate's administrator or executor is not a family member, or if the court deems it necessary, a bond may be required. A bond ensures that the estate is administered properly and protects the estate from mismanagement. This cost can vary widely based on the estate's size.

2. Time Costs of Probate

In addition to the financial burden, probate can also be very time-consuming. Depending on the complexity of the estate, it can take anywhere from six months to several years to complete the probate process.

- **Time to Appoint an Executor**: Once the will is filed, it can take time for the court to officially appoint an executor or administrator. This step can take weeks or even months.
- **Inventory and Valuation**: Gathering all the assets and determining their value is a time-consuming process. If the estate includes real estate, multiple bank accounts, investments, and personal property, this step can take a long time.
- **Paying Debts and Taxes**: Settling debts, paying taxes, and resolving any legal claims can take several months or even years, depending on the complexity of the estate.
- **Disputes Among Family Members**: If there is a family dispute over the will or how assets should be distributed, this can lead to lengthy court battles, extending the probate process even further.

For families already dealing with the loss of a loved one, the emotional toll of a drawn-out probate process can be significant. The longer probate takes, the longer family members must wait for closure, making it more difficult for them to move on.

The Role of Probate in Estate Planning

In estate planning, probate plays a central role. Understanding how probate works helps you make informed decisions about how to plan your estate in a way that minimizes its impact on your loved ones. While probate is a necessary process for many estates, it is not always the most efficient way to handle the distribution of assets, especially if your goal is to reduce costs and time delays for your family.

Probate and Your Estate Plan: The role of probate in your estate plan depends on the type of plan you create. If your plan includes only a will, your estate will almost certainly have to go through probate. However, if your estate plan includes a living trust, your assets can bypass probate, which will save your loved ones both time and money.

Here are a few ways probate impacts your estate plan:

- **Assets Not in a Trust:** One of the biggest issues with probate is that it only applies to assets that are solely in the name of the deceased. If the deceased did not use a living trust or did not properly fund their trust, those assets must go through probate.
- **Wills and Probate:** When you write a will, you're essentially leaving instructions for the court to follow. Your will specifies who should receive your property after your death, but it does not avoid the probate process. In fact, the will must be validated through probate before your assets can be distributed to your heirs.
- **Living Trusts and Probate:** A living trust, on the other hand, is specifically designed to avoid probate. With a trust, assets are transferred into the trust during the grantor's lifetime, so upon death, they can be distributed without the need for court involvement. This saves time, money, and avoids the public nature of probate proceedings.

The living trust is often considered the most effective tool to avoid probate. However, creating a trust alone doesn't guarantee the avoidance of probate. All of your assets must be properly transferred into the trust during your lifetime, or they may still be subject to probate.

How to Avoid Probate

If your goal is to minimize or avoid probate altogether, there are several strategies that can help you achieve this. Below are some of the most effective ways to plan your estate in a way that bypasses the probate process.

1. Create a Living Trust

As discussed earlier, one of the primary reasons people create living trusts is to avoid probate. By transferring your assets into the trust, you can ensure that they are managed by your designated trustee after your death without the need for probate court intervention. The trust must be properly funded, meaning all your assets (real estate, bank accounts, investments, etc.) must be transferred into the trust during your lifetime.

2. Joint Ownership of Property

Joint ownership of property with rights of survivorship is another way to avoid probate. If two or more people own property jointly, upon the death of one owner, the property automatically passes to the surviving owner(s) without the need for probate. This applies to real estate, bank accounts, and other assets. However, be cautious with this method, as it may not be appropriate in all situations, particularly if the joint owner is not someone you fully trust or if you don't want them to inherit everything.

3. Beneficiary Designations

Many financial accounts, such as retirement accounts (401(k)s, IRAs), life insurance policies, and bank accounts, allow you to designate beneficiaries. When you pass away, these assets automatically transfer to the named beneficiaries, bypassing probate. It's essential to review and update beneficiary designations regularly to ensure they align with your estate plan.

4. Transfer-on-Death (TOD) and Payable-on-Death (POD) Accounts

Some states allow you to designate a beneficiary for certain types of assets, such as real estate (transfer-on-death) or bank accounts (payable-on-death). These accounts pass directly to the beneficiary upon your death without going through probate. These designations are relatively simple to set up and are a great way to avoid probate for specific assets.

Why a Living Trust Prevents Probate

A **living trust** is one of the most powerful tools in estate planning, particularly when it comes to **avoiding probate**. Understanding how a living trust prevents probate requires a deep dive into the mechanics of how both probate and living trusts function. To do this, let's first look at what probate is and how a living trust works.

Probate Process Overview

When someone dies, their estate must go through **probate** unless certain steps are taken to avoid it. Probate is the legal process through which a court verifies the authenticity of a deceased person's will (if one exists), identifies and appraises the decedent's assets, pays off any debts and taxes, and finally distributes the remaining assets to the beneficiaries or heirs. This process often takes months or even years, depending on the complexity of the estate.

During probate, **everything becomes public record**, including details about the deceased person's assets, liabilities, and how the property is to be distributed. This makes probate not only time-consuming and costly, but it can also lead to unwanted scrutiny and potential family disputes.

Now, let's examine how a living trust prevents probate:

1. **Avoiding Court Involvement**

   A living trust is a legal document that allows you to place your assets into a trust while you are alive. As the trust's creator (also called the grantor or settlor), you appoint yourself as the trustee, meaning you can manage your assets as you always have during your lifetime. However, upon your death, the control of your assets doesn't need to go through the probate court. Instead, the assets pass directly to the named beneficiaries through the trust.

The **trustee**, whom you've chosen, steps in to manage and distribute the assets according to the terms laid out in the trust. Since the trust has already "owned" the property, there's no need for a court to validate its terms or decide on asset distribution. This saves time, avoids public scrutiny, and prevents the delays caused by the probate process.

1. **No Probate for Trust Assets**

    One of the biggest advantages of a living trust is that **assets held within the trust** bypass the probate process entirely. As long as the property is properly titled in the name of the trust during your lifetime, those assets do not have to go through probate. This is in stark contrast to a traditional will, where the assets must be probated before they can be distributed.

For example, if you own a home and transfer the title to the living trust, the home will pass directly to your beneficiaries after you die, without the need for court intervention.

1. **Seamless Transfer of Assets**

    When assets are in a living trust, their transfer to heirs can be **immediate** and **efficient**. Since the trust is already in place, it provides clear instructions for the successor trustee on how to manage and distribute the property. This can be especially useful for real estate or business interests, where time-sensitive actions are often necessary.

For example, if your estate includes real property (like a family home or investment properties), the trustee can immediately take action to transfer ownership to the beneficiaries without having to wait for the court's approval. This eliminates one of the primary issues with probate, which is the delay in asset distribution.

1. **Privacy of Estate Affairs**

    Unlike a will that is a public document once it goes through probate, a living trust remains private. Probate proceedings are **open to the public**, meaning anyone can access the details of your will and estate.

On the other hand, because a living trust does not involve the court (except in rare cases where legal challenges arise), the assets and instructions in a living trust remain **private**, protecting your family's financial matters from public view.

1. **Cost Savings**

While setting up a living trust may require legal assistance and upfront costs, the costs of probate can quickly outweigh the initial setup cost of a trust. Probate often involves significant **court fees**, **attorney fees**, and **executor fees**, all of which come from the estate. These costs can significantly reduce the assets available to your beneficiaries. By avoiding probate, the estate can save substantial sums in administrative fees.

1. **Incapacity Planning**

A living trust also includes a provision for your **incapacity**. If you become mentally or physically incapacitated and are unable to manage your own affairs, the successor trustee you've chosen can step in and manage the trust assets for you, according to your instructions. In this way, a living trust acts as a seamless continuation of management, ensuring that there is no need for court intervention to appoint a conservator or guardian. This feature also prevents potential delays and confusion, making it a valuable tool for both incapacity and death.

How Probate Can Affect Your Family's Future

Probate doesn't just affect the immediate handling of your estate; it can have long-term effects on your family's emotional, financial, and legal future. Here's how the probate process can affect your loved ones:

1. Emotional Toll on Family Members

Losing a loved one is already an emotional challenge. When the probate process drags on for months or even years, it can compound the grief and stress your family members are experiencing. They may feel stuck, unable to move forward or get closure, particularly if the probate process becomes contentious or if disagreements arise among family members over asset distribution.

If there are multiple heirs or beneficiaries, probate can ignite conflict, as everyone waits to receive their portion of the estate. This can create tension and potentially lead to permanent rifts within the family. The public nature of probate can also lead to personal details being exposed, causing embarrassment and further complicating the grieving process.

2. Financial Burden on Heirs

Probate often comes with a financial cost that can reduce the inheritance your family members receive. These costs can include:

- **Court Fees**: Many courts charge filing fees, and these can add up quickly.
- **Attorney Fees**: Since probate is a legal process, many estates hire attorneys to navigate the system. These fees can become particularly high in complex estates, especially if disagreements or disputes arise.
- **Executor Fees**: The person appointed to manage the estate (the executor) is entitled to compensation. This fee is typically based on the value of the estate, further reducing the amount available to heirs.

These fees must be paid before the estate can be distributed, meaning that the money and assets left behind for your loved ones could be significantly reduced. This financial strain can impact the well-being of the heirs, especially if the estate includes only modest assets.

3. Delays in Asset Distribution

The probate process often takes a long time—sometimes even years—before assets are fully distributed to the beneficiaries. This can delay the inheritance of properties, money, or other valuables, and in some cases, beneficiaries may find themselves waiting for assets that they need immediately.

For instance, if a family relies on the sale of a house or other property to cover living expenses, the long probate process may prevent them from accessing the funds they need quickly. Probate can also delay the management of business interests or investments, creating challenges for surviving family members who need to make critical financial decisions.

4. Public Disclosure of Family Affairs

One of the most overlooked consequences of probate is the **public nature** of the process. Since probate involves a court, all proceedings and documents filed with the court are public records. This means that the details of your will, your assets, and your beneficiaries become accessible to anyone interested in them.

For families who value privacy, this is a major concern. The disclosure of personal and financial information can be uncomfortable and sometimes damaging, particularly if there are conflicts within the family over asset distribution or if the estate includes significant wealth or complicated financial matters. The privacy that a living trust provides is a major advantage over the probate process in this respect.

5. Risk of Mistakes and Disputes

Probate is an administrative process, and like any process that involves multiple parties and complex rules, it's prone to errors and mistakes. If something goes wrong, it could further delay the process or even result in a costly legal battle. Additionally, if someone challenges the will—whether because they believe the deceased was not of sound mind or because they feel entitled to more than what was left to them—it can lead to lengthy legal disputes that further drain resources and sour family relationships.

This risk of disputes is one of the reasons why many people choose to use a living trust instead of a will. A trust is less likely to be contested than a will because it does not go through probate, and the terms of the trust are usually clearer and more difficult to challenge.

Chapter 3: The Anatomy of a Living Trust

What a Living Trust Is and How It Works

A **living trust**, also known as an **inter vivos trust**, is a legal document that allows you to place your assets in a trust during your lifetime. Unlike a will, which comes into effect only after death, a living trust takes effect as soon as it is created and funded, meaning the assets in the trust are managed according to your instructions during your life and distributed to your beneficiaries after your death.

Key Components of a Living Trust

A living trust involves three key parties:

1. **The Grantor (or Settlor)**: This is the person who creates the trust and transfers their assets into it. The grantor has complete control over the trust while alive and can amend or revoke the trust as needed.
2. **The Trustee**: The trustee is responsible for managing the assets in the trust. The grantor typically serves as the trustee during their lifetime, but they can designate a successor trustee to take over upon their death or incapacity. The trustee's role is to follow the instructions of the trust and ensure that the assets are managed and distributed in accordance with the grantor's wishes.
3. **The Beneficiaries**: These are the individuals or organizations that will ultimately receive the trust's assets after the grantor's death or incapacity. Beneficiaries can include family members, charities, or other entities.

How a Living Trust Works

Once a living trust is created, the grantor transfers ownership of their assets to the trust. This means the trust "owns" the assets, not the individual. While the grantor is alive and mentally competent, they retain full control over the assets in the trust, and can modify, add, or remove assets as they choose.

- **During the Grantor's Lifetime**: The trust is active, and the grantor (as the trustee) can manage the assets, sell property, invest, and make withdrawals as desired.
- **If the Grantor Becomes Incapacitated**: If the grantor is unable to manage their affairs due to illness or incapacity, the successor trustee, who was appointed when the trust was created, steps in and manages the assets on the grantor's behalf. This eliminates the need for a court-appointed guardian or conservator, which can be a lengthy and costly process.
- **Upon the Grantor's Death**: When the grantor passes away, the successor trustee takes over the management of the trust. The assets are distributed according to the instructions set out in the trust document. Since the assets are already titled in the name of the trust, the trust does not go through probate, ensuring a much quicker and more private distribution to the beneficiaries.

This ability to transfer assets quickly and privately is one of the most significant benefits of a living trust. Unlike a will, which requires probate to be validated before assets can be distributed, a living trust allows for **immediate** asset distribution according to the grantor's wishes, bypassing the entire probate process.

The Different Types of Trusts: Which One Is Right for You?

While a **revocable living trust** is one of the most common types, it is not the only type of trust available. There are many different types of trusts, each designed for specific purposes. To select the best trust for your situation, it's essential to understand the various options and what they offer.

1. Revocable Living Trust

The **revocable living trust** is the most popular type of living trust and the one most commonly used in estate planning. The main feature of a revocable trust is that the grantor has the ability to change or revoke the trust at any time during their lifetime, as long as they are mentally competent.

Benefits:

- **Flexibility**: The grantor can amend or revoke the trust as circumstances change (e.g., after marriage, divorce, or the birth of a child).
- **Avoids Probate**: The assets placed in the trust avoid probate, ensuring a quicker and more efficient transfer to beneficiaries after the grantor's death.
- **Incapacity Planning**: A revocable living trust allows for a seamless transition of management if the grantor becomes incapacitated, avoiding the need for guardianship or conservatorship.

Limitations:

- **No Tax Benefits**: Since the grantor retains control over the trust and can revoke it, the assets in a revocable trust are treated as part of the grantor's estate for tax purposes. This means there are no immediate tax benefits.

2. Irrevocable Living Trust

An **irrevocable living trust** differs from a revocable trust in that the grantor cannot change or revoke it once it has been created and assets have been transferred into it. This type of trust is often used for **asset protection**, **tax savings**, and **estate tax reduction**.

Benefits:

- **Asset Protection**: Because the grantor no longer owns the assets once they are transferred to an irrevocable trust, the assets are generally protected from creditors, lawsuits, and other claims.
- **Estate Tax Benefits**: Irrevocable trusts can help reduce the value of the grantor's taxable estate, potentially lowering estate taxes upon death.
- **Tax Benefits**: Income generated by the trust may be taxed to the trust itself, rather than the grantor, which may offer tax advantages.

Limitations:

- **No Flexibility**: Once assets are transferred into an irrevocable trust, the grantor cannot change the terms or regain control over the assets. This can be a disadvantage if circumstances change.
- **Complexity**: Setting up and managing an irrevocable trust requires careful planning, and it may be more complex and costly than a revocable living trust.

3. Testamentary Trust

A **testamentary trust** is a type of trust that is created through a will and comes into effect only after the grantor's death. This type of trust does not avoid probate, as it is funded and activated by the probate court after the will is validated.

Benefits:

- **Control Over Distribution**: It allows the grantor to control how and when assets are distributed after death, which can be useful if the beneficiaries are minors or not financially responsible.

- **Flexibility**: It can be customized to address specific goals, such as providing for the care of minor children or disabled family members.

Limitations:

- **Probate Involvement**: Since it is created through a will, a testamentary trust must go through probate, which means it will be subject to court approval and public disclosure.

4. Charitable Remainder Trust

A **charitable remainder trust (CRT)** is designed to provide income to the grantor or beneficiaries during their lifetime, with the remaining assets going to a charity after the grantor's death. This trust is often used for individuals who want to leave a charitable legacy while also receiving income from the trust.

Benefits:

- **Tax Deduction**: The grantor can receive a charitable tax deduction for the portion of the trust that is designated to charity.
- **Income for Beneficiaries**: The trust can provide income to the grantor or other beneficiaries during their lifetime.
- **Estate Tax Reduction**: The portion of the trust designated to charity is removed from the estate, potentially reducing estate taxes.

Limitations:

- **Irrevocable**: Like other irrevocable trusts, a charitable remainder trust cannot be changed once established, and the grantor relinquishes control of the assets in the trust.

5. Special Needs Trust

A **special needs trust** is designed to provide for a disabled beneficiary without affecting their eligibility for government benefits, such as Medicaid or Supplemental Security Income (SSI).

Benefits:

- **Maintains Eligibility for Government Benefits**: A special needs trust allows the beneficiary to receive funds from the trust without disqualifying them from public assistance programs.
- **Protects Assets for Care**: It ensures that the beneficiary will have access to funds for their care, in addition to the government benefits they receive.

Limitations:

- **Strict Guidelines**: Special needs trusts must be set up according to specific rules to ensure the beneficiary's eligibility for government benefits is maintained.

How to Choose the Best Trust for Your Needs

Choosing the best type of trust for your needs depends on several factors, including your goals, the complexity of your estate, your family situation, and your financial concerns. Here are some steps to help you decide which trust is right for you:

1. **Consider Your Estate Planning Goals**

   Are you trying to avoid probate? Do you need tax savings or asset protection? Are you planning to leave a charitable legacy? Your goals will influence which trust you should use. For example, if you want to avoid probate and maintain control over your assets during your lifetime, a **revocable living trust** might be the best option. If you need asset protection and want to reduce estate taxes, an **irrevocable living trust** may be the better choice.

1. **Evaluate Your Family's Needs**

   If you have minor children, a special needs beneficiary, or beneficiaries who may not be financially responsible, you might consider a trust that offers specific provisions for those situations. A **testamentary trust** or a **special needs trust** might be necessary depending on your family's unique needs.

1. **Think About Asset Protection**

   If protecting your assets from creditors, lawsuits, or divorce is important, you may want to consider an **irrevocable trust**. An irrevocable trust can shield your assets from outside claims, providing peace of mind knowing that your assets will be protected.

1. **Work with an Estate Planning Attorney**

The best way to ensure that you select the right trust for your needs is to work with an experienced estate planning attorney. They can help you navigate the complexities of trusts, explain the tax implications, and ensure that your estate plan is set up according to your goals and state laws.

The Key Components of a Living Trust

A **living trust** is a legal tool used in estate planning to help manage and distribute your assets while avoiding the lengthy and costly process of probate. Understanding the key components of a living trust is essential for ensuring that it serves its purpose effectively. At its core, a living trust consists of several key elements that work together to ensure your wishes are honored during your lifetime and after your death.

Here are the key components of a living trust:

1. The Trust Document

The primary component of a living trust is the **trust document** itself. This document outlines the details of the trust, including the terms of the trust, the assets placed into it, and how those assets are to be managed and distributed. The trust document is legally binding and serves as the foundation for the entire trust. It must be carefully drafted to reflect the grantor's intentions, and it must comply with state laws to be enforceable.

The trust document should address the following:

- **The Purpose of the Trust**: The trust document should state the reasons for creating the trust, whether it's to avoid probate, minimize estate taxes, provide for loved ones, or any combination of these reasons.
- **The Instructions for Distribution**: It outlines how the trust's assets should be distributed to beneficiaries upon the grantor's death or incapacity. This includes specifying when and under what circumstances the assets are to be distributed, and whether the distribution is to be made in installments or as a lump sum.
- **Terms for Modifying or Revoking the Trust**: If the trust is revocable, the document should include provisions for how the trust can be modified or revoked during the grantor's lifetime. For example, if the grantor's circumstances change (e.g., a marriage, divorce, or birth of children), the trust should have flexibility to

adjust accordingly.

2. The Grantor (or Settlor)

The **grantor**, also known as the **settlor** or **trustor**, is the individual who creates and funds the trust. The grantor's role is central to the living trust. The grantor transfers assets into the trust and specifies how those assets will be managed, used, and distributed. In most cases, the grantor serves as the **trustee** during their lifetime, managing their assets according to their wishes.

The grantor must have the legal capacity to create the trust, meaning they must be of sound mind and not under duress. Additionally, the grantor should carefully consider what assets to place into the trust and ensure that the transfer of those assets is done correctly to avoid probate. The grantor may choose to remain the trustee as long as they are mentally and physically capable, or they may designate a successor trustee to take over in case of incapacity.

3. The Trustee

The **trustee** is the individual or institution responsible for managing the trust's assets according to the terms set out in the trust document. The trustee is a fiduciary, meaning they are legally obligated to act in the best interests of the beneficiaries and to carry out the instructions provided by the grantor.

The trustee's role is important because they are responsible for overseeing the trust's operations and ensuring the assets are properly managed. The trustee may have several responsibilities, including:

- **Managing Trust Assets**: The trustee is responsible for ensuring that the trust's assets are properly managed, including investments, real estate, and personal property.
- **Making Distributions**: The trustee is responsible for distributing assets to the beneficiaries as specified in the trust document. This may include paying for the beneficiary's education, medical care, or other specified expenses.
- **Filing Taxes**: The trustee may also be responsible for filing taxes for the trust and paying any taxes owed from the trust's assets. This includes income taxes on the trust's earnings and estate taxes upon

the death of the grantor.

- **Keeping Records**: The trustee must maintain accurate records of all transactions involving the trust's assets. These records should be available to beneficiaries and, if necessary, the court.

4. The Successor Trustee

The **successor trustee** is the person or entity designated to take over the trustee's duties upon the grantor's death or incapacity. The successor trustee will step in if the grantor becomes incapacitated and will take over full responsibility after the grantor's death. It is crucial to choose a successor trustee who is trustworthy, reliable, and capable of managing the trust effectively.

If the grantor becomes incapacitated, the successor trustee will assume control of the trust's assets and will manage them for the benefit of the grantor (if still alive) or the beneficiaries (after the grantor's death). The successor trustee must follow the terms of the trust document and carry out the grantor's wishes as outlined in the document.

5. The Beneficiaries

The **beneficiaries** are the individuals or organizations that will receive the trust's assets. The grantor designates the beneficiaries in the trust document and can specify how and when they will receive distributions from the trust. Beneficiaries can be family members, friends, charities, or other entities.

The trust document should provide clear instructions on how the assets will be distributed. For example, the trust may specify that beneficiaries will receive a certain amount of money or property upon the grantor's death, or it may specify that distributions are to be made over time (e.g., monthly, annually) or upon the occurrence of a specific event (such as reaching a certain age).

6. The Trust Property (Assets)

The **trust property**, also known as **trust assets**, includes everything that is transferred into the trust by the grantor. These assets can include cash, real estate, investments, business interests, jewelry, art, or any other property the grantor wishes to include.

For a living trust to be effective, it is essential that the assets are properly transferred into the trust during the grantor's lifetime. This involves retitling assets in the name of the trust (e.g., transferring real estate deeds, bank accounts, investment portfolios, etc.). If the assets are not properly transferred into the trust, they may still be subject to probate, defeating the purpose of the trust.

The Role of Trustees and Beneficiaries

The success of a living trust depends heavily on the **trustees** and **beneficiaries** and the roles they play in ensuring that the trust's terms are carried out as intended. Let's take a closer look at their roles.

The Role of the Trustee

As mentioned earlier, the trustee is the person or entity responsible for managing the trust's assets and ensuring that the instructions in the trust document are followed. The role of the trustee is critical to the trust's success, as they are legally bound to act in the best interest of the beneficiaries and carry out the grantor's wishes.

Here are the key duties of a trustee:

1. **Fiduciary Duty**: The trustee has a fiduciary responsibility to act in the best interest of the beneficiaries. This means they must manage the trust's assets responsibly, avoid conflicts of interest, and ensure that all actions taken align with the trust document's provisions.
2. **Asset Management**: The trustee must manage the trust's assets, including investments, real estate, and personal property, in a way that protects and grows the value of the estate. This includes making decisions about investments, selling property, and ensuring that the trust remains financially sound.
3. **Distribute Assets According to the Trust's Terms**: The trustee is responsible for distributing assets to the beneficiaries as specified in the trust document. This includes following the instructions on timing, amounts, and conditions for distribution. For example, if the trust provides that a beneficiary will receive a distribution at a certain age, the trustee must ensure that this happens.
4. **Tax Filing and Reporting**: The trustee must file tax returns for the trust, pay any taxes owed, and keep accurate records of all financial transactions. This is a critical responsibility, as failing to meet tax obligations can result in penalties or interest charges.
5. **Accountability**: The trustee must provide regular reports to the

beneficiaries, showing how the trust's assets are being managed and whether any distributions have been made. Transparency is key to ensuring that the trustee is acting in the best interest of the beneficiaries.

The Role of the Beneficiaries

The **beneficiaries** are the individuals or organizations who stand to benefit from the trust. The role of the beneficiaries is largely passive; they receive the trust's assets according to the terms set out in the trust document.

However, beneficiaries do have certain rights:

1. **Right to Receive Distributions**: Beneficiaries are entitled to receive distributions from the trust according to the trust document. This could include receiving money, property, or other assets.
2. **Right to Be Informed**: While the trustee is not obligated to provide detailed reports on a day-to-day basis, beneficiaries have the right to be informed about the trust's assets and how they are being managed. If the beneficiaries believe that the trustee is not fulfilling their duties properly, they have the right to request an accounting or even take legal action in some cases.
3. **Right to Challenge the Trust**: Beneficiaries can challenge the trust if they believe that the terms are not being followed or that the trustee is acting improperly. This could include situations where there are disputes about the distribution of assets or the validity of the trust itself. However, challenging a trust is typically a lengthy and costly process.

Chapter 4: The 5 Must-Have Clauses for Your Living Trust

1. The Trust's Purpose and Objectives Clause

The first clause that should be included in your living trust is a **Purpose and Objectives Clause**. This clause is crucial because it clearly outlines the overall goals of the trust and the grantor's intentions. By stating the purpose of the trust in clear and concise language, you set the stage for how the trustee should act and what they should prioritize.

Why It's Important

The Purpose and Objectives Clause helps to prevent misunderstandings and provides guidance for the trustee. While a living trust generally exists to avoid probate, distribute assets, and provide for loved ones, every trust has unique considerations based on the grantor's specific needs. For example, the objectives could include:

- Avoiding probate and minimizing delays in the transfer of assets.
- Ensuring that beneficiaries are provided for according to the grantor's wishes.
- Managing the grantor's property during incapacity and after death.
- Providing for special needs beneficiaries without affecting their eligibility for government benefits.

What to Include

In this clause, the grantor should include:

- **The overall goal** of the trust (e.g., avoiding probate, protecting assets, providing for loved ones, charitable giving).
- **Any special instructions or provisions** that the trustee should be aware of (e.g., taking care of a dependent child, managing family business interests, or handling pets).
- **The distribution of assets**: This includes any specific bequests (e.g., specific items or amounts of money) to designated beneficiaries.

A clear, specific statement of purpose helps the trustee understand their role and ensures they act in line with the grantor's intentions.

2. The Successor Trustee Clause

One of the most important decisions you make when setting up a living trust is who will serve as the **trustee.** The **Successor Trustee Clause** designates who will take over the management of the trust in the event that the original trustee (usually the grantor) becomes incapacitated or dies. This clause outlines the process of selecting a successor trustee and their responsibilities.

Why It's Important

This clause is critical for ensuring continuity of asset management and distribution. If a successor trustee is not clearly named, or if the successor trustee's duties are not well-defined, the trust may face significant delays or legal challenges. A successor trustee must be able to handle financial responsibilities, legal matters, and family dynamics. They should be someone who is trustworthy, organized, and capable of fulfilling the responsibilities of managing the trust.

What to Include

The Successor Trustee Clause should address the following:

- **Designation of Successor Trustees**: This clause should name at least one successor trustee and may also list alternate trustees in case the primary successor trustee is unable or unwilling to serve.
- **Trustee Powers and Responsibilities**: Clearly define what powers the successor trustee will have (e.g., managing assets, paying debts, distributing property to beneficiaries).
- **Incapacity Provisions**: Include a provision for when a trustee can no longer serve due to incapacity. This ensures that the trust's affairs can be managed seamlessly even if the original trustee becomes mentally or physically incapacitated.

Example of a Successor Trustee Clause:

"If I become incapacitated or pass away, I hereby appoint [Name of Successor Trustee] as the successor trustee of this trust. In the event that [Successor Trustee] is unable or unwilling to serve, I designate [Alternate

Successor Trustee] to take over the responsibilities of managing and distributing the trust."

3. The Distribution Clause

The **Distribution Clause** is the heart of your living trust. This clause specifies how and when your assets will be distributed to the beneficiaries. The distribution of assets can be complex, so it's essential to be as specific as possible to avoid confusion or conflict.

Why It's Important

One of the main reasons people create a living trust is to ensure that their assets are distributed according to their wishes. The Distribution Clause ensures that your wishes are clearly understood and legally enforceable. It helps to avoid potential disputes between family members and beneficiaries, which can be common if a trust is vague or unclear about asset distribution.

What to Include

In this clause, the grantor should specify:

- **Who will receive the assets**: Clearly identify the beneficiaries, including family members, friends, charities, or other entities.
- **How assets will be distributed**: Define how assets will be divided, whether it's by percentage, specific items, or lump sums. Be clear about who gets what and when.
- **Conditions of Distribution**: Specify any conditions for distribution. For example, a beneficiary might receive their share of the inheritance only when they reach a certain age, or they may be provided with a trust for health care or educational expenses.
- **Special Instructions for Certain Assets**: If there are specific assets (such as family heirlooms or business interests) that require special handling, the Distribution Clause should specify how these items should be managed or transferred.

Example of a Distribution Clause:

"Upon my death, I direct my trustee to distribute the assets of the trust as follows:

- To [Beneficiary 1], I give [percentage] of the trust assets.

- To [Beneficiary 2], I give my [specific asset, e.g., my house or artwork].
- To [Beneficiary 3], I give a sum of $[amount] for educational purposes."

4. The Spendthrift Clause

The **Spendthrift Clause** is an important provision to include if you are concerned about the ability of your beneficiaries to manage their inheritance. This clause is designed to protect a beneficiary's inheritance from creditors and prevent them from squandering the trust's assets.

Why It's Important

If a beneficiary has financial difficulties or is prone to poor money management, a spendthrift clause can prevent them from misusing the assets in the trust. It can also protect the trust's assets from being seized by creditors in case the beneficiary faces a lawsuit or other financial issues.

What to Include

The Spendthrift Clause should:

- **Restrict the beneficiary's access** to the trust's assets for purposes other than what is stated in the trust document (e.g., health care, education, living expenses).
- **Limit creditor access**: The clause should prevent creditors from seizing the trust assets to pay off the beneficiary's debts.
- **Specify how funds can be used**: The clause should outline the conditions under which a trustee can release funds to a beneficiary and the purposes for which the funds can be used.

Example of a Spendthrift Clause:

"None of the trust assets shall be subject to the debts, liabilities, or obligations of any beneficiary. No beneficiary shall have the right to sell, assign, or transfer their interest in the trust, nor shall creditors have access to the trust assets to satisfy any debts of the beneficiary."

5. The Revocation or Amendment Clause

One of the significant features of a revocable living trust is that it can be amended or revoked at any time during the grantor's lifetime, provided they are mentally competent. The **Revocation or Amendment Clause** outlines the procedures for making changes to the trust or revoking it entirely.

Why It's Important

Life circumstances change, and your estate planning needs may evolve over time. The Revocation or Amendment Clause ensures that you retain the flexibility to modify or revoke your trust as necessary. Whether you need to change your beneficiaries, add assets, or remove a trustee, this clause gives you the legal ability to make changes without going through complicated legal processes.

What to Include

This clause should include:

- **How changes can be made**: Specify the method for modifying or amending the trust (e.g., a written document signed by the grantor).
- **Conditions for revocation**: If you wish to revoke the trust entirely, this clause should clearly state how to revoke it, ensuring that the trust can be terminated if desired.
- **Formality requirements**: Specify whether any additional steps are required for amending or revoking the trust (e.g., notarization, witnesses).

Example of a Revocation or Amendment Clause:

"The Grantor reserves the right to amend, modify, or revoke this trust, in whole or in part, at any time during their lifetime. Any amendments or modifications must be made in writing, signed by the Grantor, and witnessed by two individuals who are not beneficiaries of the trust."

Sample Clauses for Different Situations

When creating a living trust, one of the most important tasks is drafting clear and precise clauses that reflect your intentions. These clauses will dictate how your assets are distributed, who manages them, and how the trust is handled if circumstances change. To help guide you, here are **sample clauses for different situations** that are commonly included in a living trust, along with an explanation of each and why they're important.

1. Distribution of Assets Clause

The **Distribution Clause** outlines how assets should be divided among beneficiaries upon your death. It's vital to specify which assets go to whom, as well as how and when they will be distributed.

Sample Clause:

"Upon my death, my trustee shall distribute the assets of this trust as follows:

- To my daughter, [Name], I give the sum of $50,000 for her personal use.
- To my son, [Name], I give my family home located at [Address], including all furniture and contents.
- The remainder of the trust estate, after payment of debts, expenses, and taxes, shall be divided equally among my children, [Names of Children], and distributed in a manner that will allow each of them to receive their portion within six months of my death."

Explanation:

This clause makes clear who gets which assets, as well as when they will receive them. It provides instructions for both specific items (like a family home or personal funds) and the general distribution of the remainder of the estate. When you draft your trust, it's important to be specific so that your wishes are clear and can be easily followed by the trustee.

2. Spendthrift Clause

A **Spendthrift Clause** is crucial for protecting assets from beneficiaries who may not be financially responsible. It prevents beneficiaries from using trust assets to settle their debts, ensuring that the funds will only be used for the beneficiary's benefit as intended by the trust.

Sample Clause:

"None of the assets held in this trust shall be subject to the debts, obligations, or liabilities of any beneficiary, nor may they be sold, pledged, or assigned. The trustee is instructed to disburse funds to the beneficiary only for health, education, maintenance, and support needs, and shall not release more than [specific percentage] per year without the trustee's discretion. This provision is intended to protect the assets from creditors and from being mismanaged."

Explanation:

This clause ensures that trust assets are shielded from creditors, preventing beneficiaries from using the inheritance to pay off debts. It also gives the trustee authority to manage how much money can be distributed annually to ensure the funds are used responsibly and in line with the grantor's intentions.

3. Special Needs Clause

A **Special Needs Clause** ensures that a beneficiary with disabilities is provided for without disqualifying them from government assistance programs, such as Medicaid or Supplemental Security Income (SSI).

Sample Clause:

"Upon my death, if my child, [Name], is still living and has a physical or mental disability that qualifies him or her for governmental assistance, I direct that any distribution from this trust be made in a manner that will not disqualify them from such assistance. The trustee shall use the funds only for supplemental needs not covered by government programs, ensuring that no distribution jeopardizes the beneficiary's eligibility for public assistance."

Explanation:

This clause is essential for ensuring that a disabled beneficiary can still access government benefits while receiving their share of the trust's assets. It allows the trustee to make distributions specifically for supplementary needs without interfering with the beneficiary's eligibility for assistance.

4. Successor Trustee Clause

The **Successor Trustee Clause** designates a new trustee in the event that the original trustee becomes incapable of fulfilling their duties, either due to incapacity or death. The successor trustee will step in and manage the trust according to the terms established in the trust document.

Sample Clause:

"If I am unable or unwilling to serve as trustee due to incapacity or death, I hereby appoint [Successor Trustee's Name], a [Relationship to Grantor] of [Address], as my successor trustee. Should [Successor Trustee] be unable or unwilling to serve, I appoint [Alternate Successor Trustee's Name] as the successor trustee."

Explanation:

This clause ensures that the trust will always have a designated trustee, even if the original trustee cannot serve. It's important to name a successor and, if desired, an alternate, in case the first choice is unavailable. The successor trustee will then assume the role of managing the trust without needing a court-appointed administrator.

5. Incapacity Clause

The **Incapacity Clause** defines what will happen if the grantor becomes incapacitated. This clause is essential for ensuring that someone can step in and manage the trust's assets if the grantor is no longer capable of doing so.

Sample Clause:

"In the event that I become incapacitated and unable to manage my affairs, as determined by two independent physicians, I appoint [Successor Trustee's Name] to serve as my trustee. The successor trustee shall have the authority to manage my financial affairs, make health care decisions on my behalf, and make distributions from the trust as needed for my health, support, and well-being."

Explanation:

This clause ensures that the trust does not go unmanaged if the grantor is incapacitated. It allows for smooth continuation of asset management and makes sure that someone trusted is in charge of both financial and medical decisions during this time. It also helps avoid the need for a court-appointed guardian or conservator.

How to Ensure Your Trust Cannot Be Misinterpreted

Having the right clauses in place is essential to making sure your living trust operates as intended. However, it's equally important that the language used in the trust is clear and precise, leaving no room for misinterpretation. Ambiguities in the trust document can lead to confusion, disputes, and delays in administering the trust. Here are some strategies for ensuring that your living trust cannot be misinterpreted:

1. Use Clear and Specific Language

One of the most common mistakes in drafting trusts is using vague or unclear language. The trust document should be as specific as possible about what you want to happen with your assets. For example, instead of simply saying, "I leave my estate to my children," you should specify, "I leave my house located at [address] to my son, [Name], and my car to my daughter, [Name]."

The more precise you are, the less chance there is for confusion about what you intended. Additionally, use terms that are legally recognized, such as "beneficiary," "trustee," and "successor trustee," to avoid ambiguity.

2. Avoid Ambiguity in Beneficiary Designations

One of the primary sources of confusion in trust documents is unclear beneficiary designations. If there's ambiguity about who is meant to receive a particular asset, it can result in disputes among family members or delays in administration.

For example, if you leave an asset to "my children," but you have more than one child, it's essential to specify the names of your children. You could even go a step further and clarify the share each child should receive (e.g., "50% to [Name] and 50% to [Name]").

3. Provide Clear Guidelines for the Trustee

The **trustee** plays a crucial role in carrying out your wishes, so it's important to make sure that their responsibilities are well-defined. Avoid general instructions like "The trustee is responsible for managing the estate." Instead, provide detailed guidance on what the trustee should do. For example, include instructions for managing specific types of assets, such as real estate or investments.

Specify how the trustee should handle the distribution of assets, under what circumstances they should make payments to beneficiaries, and what steps they should take if they encounter challenges in fulfilling the trust.

4. Avoid Conflicting Provisions

Another reason a trust might be misinterpreted is if there are conflicting provisions. For instance, if one clause says to divide the assets equally among your children, but another clause leaves a specific asset to one child, it could lead to confusion about how to interpret your intentions.

To avoid conflicts, review the trust carefully and ensure that all provisions are aligned. If there are multiple clauses that seem to contradict each other, clarify your intentions and modify the language to resolve any discrepancies.

5. Regularly Review and Update the Trust

Circumstances change over time, and your living trust should evolve with them. If you get married, divorced, have children, or acquire new assets, you must update your trust to reflect these changes. Additionally, periodic reviews will ensure that the clauses in your trust still reflect your current wishes and that the language remains clear.

By regularly reviewing and updating your trust, you can avoid potential issues that might arise from outdated or contradictory provisions.

6. Work with an Estate Planning Professional

While it's possible to draft a living trust on your own, it's highly recommended that you work with an **estate planning attorney**. An attorney will ensure that your trust is legally sound, uses the appropriate language, and reflects your intentions clearly. They can also help you avoid mistakes and pitfalls that might lead to confusion or disputes later on.

Chapter 5: Building Your Living Trust: A Step-by-Step Guide

Preparing to Create Your Living Trust: What You Need to Know

Before you begin creating your living trust, there are several important pieces of information you need to gather. Preparing for this process involves understanding the role of the trust, the decisions you'll need to make, and the specific instructions you want to include in the trust document.

What Is a Living Trust?

A living trust is a legal document that allows you to place your assets into a trust during your lifetime. You, as the **grantor**, create the trust, transfer your assets into it, and designate a **trustee** to manage the assets on your behalf. After your death or incapacity, the assets in the trust are distributed to your **beneficiaries** according to the instructions outlined in the trust.

A living trust has several key benefits:

- **Avoidance of probate**: Since the assets are owned by the trust and not you personally, they do not need to go through the probate process after your death.
- **Privacy**: Unlike a will, which becomes a public document when probated, a living trust remains private.
- **Incapacity planning**: If you become incapacitated, the trustee can step in to manage the trust assets without needing court intervention.

However, before you can enjoy these benefits, you must ensure that the trust is properly created and funded, and that the key decisions are made clearly and effectively.

Key Decisions You Will Make in Creating Your Trust

Creating a living trust involves a few key decisions:

1. **Who will be your trustee?**
2. **Who will be your beneficiaries?**
3. **What assets will you include in the trust?**
4. **How will the assets be distributed to beneficiaries?**

Step 1: Choosing Your Trustees and Beneficiaries

Choosing Your Trustees

The **trustee** is the person or institution responsible for managing the assets in your trust according to your instructions. One of the most critical decisions you will make is selecting the right trustee.

Your trustee will have a fiduciary duty to act in the best interests of the beneficiaries, following the terms of the trust. It is essential to choose someone who is trustworthy, responsible, and capable of handling financial matters. You can choose an individual or a financial institution (such as a bank or trust company) to serve as your trustee.

Here's what to consider when choosing your trustee:

1. **Trustworthiness**: The trustee will have control over your assets, so it is essential to choose someone you trust to act in your best interests. Consider individuals who have demonstrated integrity and reliability in their personal or professional lives.
2. **Financial Responsibility**: The trustee must be capable of managing your estate and finances, especially if your assets are substantial or complex (such as real estate or business interests). It is important to choose someone with basic financial knowledge or who has access to the resources necessary to manage the estate.
3. **Ability to Follow Instructions**: The trustee will need to understand and follow your wishes as laid out in the trust document. Choose someone who is detail-oriented and can handle the responsibilities of administering the trust without unnecessary delays or complications.
4. **Capacity to Serve**: Consider whether the person you're appointing will be able to serve as trustee in the long term. It's essential to choose someone who will be around to fulfill this role and who is capable of doing so, especially in the event of your incapacity.
5. **Consider a Successor Trustee**: You'll also want to name a **successor trustee**, who will step in if your primary trustee is unable or unwilling to serve. It's important to select someone who is capable of stepping

into the role without causing disruption to the management of the trust.

Example Clause for Trustee:

"If I am unable to serve as trustee, I appoint [Name] as successor trustee. If [Name] is unable or unwilling to serve, I appoint [Alternate Name] as successor trustee."

Choosing Your Beneficiaries

Beneficiaries are the people or organizations that will receive your assets after your death. Deciding who will benefit from your trust is one of the most personal decisions in estate planning. You can designate family members, friends, charities, or other entities as beneficiaries.

Here's what to consider when choosing your beneficiaries:

1. **Family and Loved Ones**: The most common beneficiaries of a living trust are family members—spouses, children, grandchildren, or other relatives. It's important to decide how much each beneficiary will receive, whether you want to divide assets equally, or whether you want to allocate different amounts based on their needs or relationship with you.
2. **Charities**: If you wish to leave a legacy, you can also include charities as beneficiaries of your trust. This can be an effective way to make a charitable donation without the need for probate, while also ensuring that your favorite causes are supported.
3. **Special Needs Beneficiaries**: If you have beneficiaries with special needs, consider creating a **special needs trust** within your living trust to ensure they are provided for without affecting their eligibility for government assistance.
4. **Contingent Beneficiaries**: You may also want to name **contingent beneficiaries**—people who will inherit your assets if your primary beneficiaries are unable or unwilling to accept the inheritance.
5. **Asset-Specific Beneficiaries**: You can also designate specific assets for specific beneficiaries. For example, you could leave your home to one child and a sum of money to another.

Example Clause for Beneficiaries:

"Upon my death, I direct my trustee to distribute the assets of my trust as follows:

- To [Beneficiary 1], I give [percentage or asset description].
- To [Beneficiary 2], I give [percentage or asset description].
- The remainder of my estate shall be divided equally among my children."

Step 2: Listing Your Assets and Valuing Them

The next crucial step in creating your living trust is compiling a comprehensive **inventory of assets**. This step is essential for ensuring that all your important assets are properly transferred into the trust and that the trust is funded correctly.

Why Listing and Valuing Assets Is Important

To ensure that your living trust functions as intended, **all assets** you want the trust to control must be legally transferred into the trust. This includes everything from **real estate** to **bank accounts**, **investments**, **personal property**, and any other valuable assets. The goal is to ensure that upon your death, the assets are in the name of the trust, allowing your trustee to handle them without the need for probate.

Additionally, it's important to know the value of your assets to ensure accurate estate planning and avoid issues with tax reporting. A proper valuation helps the trustee administer the estate fairly and effectively, especially when it comes to distributing assets or paying any taxes or debts associated with the estate.

How to List Your Assets

Start by identifying **all assets** you own or control. This includes:

- **Real Estate**: Any property you own, including your primary residence, vacation homes, rental properties, and land.
- **Financial Accounts**: This includes bank accounts, investment accounts (stocks, bonds, mutual funds), retirement accounts (IRAs, 401(k)s), and certificates of deposit.
- **Personal Property**: Tangible personal property such as vehicles, jewelry, art, collectibles, and family heirlooms.
- **Life Insurance Policies**: Include any life insurance policies where the trust will be the beneficiary or where you may want to leave specific instructions regarding the proceeds.

- **Business Interests**: If you own a business, include ownership interest in corporations, partnerships, LLCs, and other entities.
- **Digital Assets**: This includes online accounts, cryptocurrencies, websites, and intellectual property that you wish to pass on to your beneficiaries.

Valuing Your Assets

Once you've listed all of your assets, you need to determine their **value**. This is a crucial step in the estate planning process, as it helps your trustee understand the total value of the trust and ensures that all debts, taxes, and distributions are handled appropriately.

- **Real Estate**: Have a professional appraisal or market analysis conducted to determine the value of any real estate in the trust.
- **Financial Accounts**: For financial accounts such as bank and investment accounts, the current balance or value can usually be found on recent statements. For non-liquid assets, you may need to hire a professional appraiser.
- **Personal Property**: Items like jewelry or art should be appraised by an expert to ensure their value is properly recorded.
- **Business Interests**: Valuing business interests often requires a business valuation expert, especially if the business is privately held or involves complex ownership structures.
- **Digital Assets**: Determine the value of any digital assets by accounting for current market prices or evaluating intellectual property such as patents, trademarks, and copyrights.

Example of Asset Listing and Valuation Clause

"In accordance with the terms of this trust, I hereby list the following assets that are to be transferred into the trust:

- My primary residence located at [address], valued at [$amount].
- My checking account at [Bank Name], with an account number of [XXXX], valued at [$amount].

- My investment account with [Brokerage Firm Name], valued at [$amount].
- My antique furniture collection, valued at [$amount]."

Step 3: Funding Your Trust: How to Transfer Assets

Funding your living trust is arguably the most critical step in the entire process of creating a trust. A living trust only works if the **assets** you want to include are properly transferred into it. If you neglect this step, your assets may still be subject to probate, defeating the purpose of creating the trust in the first place.

When you create a living trust, you must legally transfer ownership of your assets to the trust. This process is called "funding" the trust. It's important to remember that without properly funding your trust, it will not avoid probate for the assets you intend to pass on.

What Assets Should Be Transferred into the Trust?

Any asset that you wish to avoid probate should be transferred into your living trust. Here are the common types of assets that should be included:

1. **Real Estate**: If you own real property (e.g., your home, rental properties, vacation homes, or land), you need to transfer the title of those properties to the trust. This is done by drafting and recording a **deed** that names the trust as the owner.
2. **Bank Accounts**: For savings and checking accounts, you need to update the account registration so that the trust is listed as the account holder. Some banks may require specific forms to accomplish this.
3. **Investment Accounts**: This includes stocks, bonds, mutual funds, and retirement accounts. Investment accounts should be retitled in the name of the trust, or, in the case of retirement accounts like 401(k)s or IRAs, you may need to name the trust as the **beneficiary**.
4. **Personal Property**: This category includes items such as jewelry, artwork, collectibles, and vehicles. For items of significant value, you may need to create a separate list that details each item and its value, which can be referenced in the trust document.
5. **Life Insurance**: You can name the trust as the beneficiary of your life insurance policy. This allows the proceeds to be paid directly to the

trust upon your death, bypassing probate.

6. **Business Interests**: If you own a business, the shares or interests in that business should be transferred to the trust. This can include partnerships, LLCs, and corporations. You may need to amend operating agreements or shareholder agreements to reflect the trust as the owner.
7. **Digital Assets**: This category includes online accounts, intellectual property, and cryptocurrencies. Depending on the nature of these assets, you may need to set up special provisions for them in your trust document.

How to Transfer Assets Into the Trust

The process of transferring assets into a trust can vary depending on the type of asset. Here's how you can transfer common assets into your trust:

1. **Real Estate**:

To transfer real estate, you must execute a **deed** (typically a **quitclaim deed** or **warranty deed**) that transfers ownership from you, as the individual, to your trust. This deed must be signed, notarized, and recorded with the county recorder's office in the county where the property is located. The deed should reference the name of the trust and include the legal description of the property.

Example:

"I, [Grantor Name], hereby transfer ownership of the real property located at [Property Address] to [Trust Name], dated [Date], as the owner of record."

1. **Bank Accounts**:

To transfer a bank account to your trust, you will typically need to present a copy of the trust agreement to your bank and request that the account be retitled in the name of the trust. Some banks will allow you to add your trust as a co-owner or designate the trust as a beneficiary of the account.

1. **Investment Accounts**:

To transfer stocks, bonds, or other investments into the trust, you will need to contact your investment firm or broker and fill out a transfer form. Depending on the type of account, the investment firm may require additional documentation to complete the transfer. You may also need to update the beneficiary designations to reflect the trust as the beneficiary.

1. **Personal Property**:

To transfer personal property, you typically don't need a formal deed. However, you should create an inventory or list of assets that are being transferred into the trust. This can include a description of valuable items such as art, jewelry, or collectibles, along with their estimated value. The list should be signed by you (the grantor) and attached to your trust document.

1. **Life Insurance**:

To make the trust the beneficiary of your life insurance policy, you need to contact your insurance company and update the beneficiary designation. It's important to ensure that the trust is named as the primary or contingent beneficiary, depending on your wishes.

1. **Business Interests**:

If you own a business, you will need to transfer ownership of the business into your trust. This may require updating business documents, such as shareholder agreements, operating agreements, or partnership agreements, to reflect the trust as the owner. If the business is a corporation, you may need to transfer shares to the trust.

1. **Digital Assets**:

Transferring digital assets such as cryptocurrency or intellectual property may require specific instructions. You should include these assets in your trust document by referencing usernames, passwords, or other access credentials. For intellectual property (such as patents, copyrights, or trademarks), you may need to assign ownership of these assets to the trust in writing.

Funding the Trust Properly

Funding the trust properly is vital for it to operate effectively. This means not only transferring ownership but also ensuring that every asset is appropriately titled in the name of the trust. Failure to fund the trust correctly means that assets outside the trust may still have to go through probate.

Step 4: Finalizing Your Trust and Making It Official

Once you have created and funded your living trust, the next step is to **finalize** the trust to ensure it is legally valid and fully effective.

What Does It Mean to Finalize Your Trust?

Finalizing your living trust means completing the legal steps necessary to make the trust official. This involves ensuring that all documents are properly executed, signed, and stored, and that your trust is legally enforceable.

Here are the steps involved in finalizing your trust:

1. **Sign the Trust Agreement**:

   The **trust agreement** must be signed by the grantor (you) in the presence of a notary public. In some cases, witnesses may also be required, depending on your state's laws. Signing the trust agreement is what officially establishes the trust.

1. **Notarization**:

   Having your trust agreement notarized ensures that the document is legally valid. A notary public will verify your identity and witness your signature. While not all states require notarization, it is strongly recommended as it can help prevent challenges to the validity of the trust in the future.

1. **Store the Trust Document Safely**:

   Once the trust document is signed, it's important to store it in a safe place. You can keep the original trust document in a secure location, such as a safe deposit box or a fireproof home safe. You should also give a copy of the trust document to your trustee, attorney, and any other key individuals involved in the management of the trust.

1. **Distribute Copies to Relevant Parties**:

It's important to give copies of the trust to the individuals who need to know about it, especially the trustee and any beneficiaries. This ensures that everyone is clear on your intentions and can act accordingly when the time comes.

1. **Update Your Will**:

Even though a living trust can handle most of your estate, it's still important to have a **pour-over will** in place. A pour-over will ensures that any assets not included in the trust (whether due to an oversight or change in circumstances) are transferred into the trust upon your death.

Common Pitfalls and How to Avoid Them

While building and funding a living trust is a straightforward process, there are common mistakes that can lead to complications down the road. Let's look at some of these potential pitfalls and how you can avoid them.

1. Failing to Fund the Trust

The most common mistake people make when setting up a living trust is failing to transfer all of their assets into the trust. If assets are left outside the trust, they may still be subject to probate. To avoid this, take the time to carefully go through each of your assets and ensure that everything is properly transferred into the trust.

How to Avoid This Pitfall:

- Make a detailed inventory of your assets.
- Work with an attorney or financial advisor to ensure all assets are titled correctly in the name of the trust.
- Review your trust regularly to ensure all new assets are included.

2. Not Naming a Successor Trustee

It's essential to name a **successor trustee** in case you are unable to manage the trust yourself due to incapacity or death. Without a successor trustee, your estate may be delayed, or the trust could be contested.

How to Avoid This Pitfall:

- Always name a primary trustee and at least one successor trustee.
- Choose someone reliable, trustworthy, and capable of managing your assets.

3. Vague Instructions for Distribution

If the instructions for distributing assets are unclear, your trust could be misinterpreted by your trustee or contested by your beneficiaries. It's essential to be as specific as possible in your distribution clauses.

How to Avoid This Pitfall:

- Be clear about who will receive what and when.
- Specify any conditions for receiving assets (e.g., age requirements or restrictions).

4. Ignoring Tax Implications

Failure to consider the tax implications of your trust could result in unexpected tax burdens for your beneficiaries or the trust itself. A living trust does not automatically reduce estate taxes or avoid income taxes.

How to Avoid This Pitfall:

- Consult with a tax professional or estate planning attorney to understand the tax implications of your trust.
- If needed, establish tax-saving strategies, such as gifting strategies or charitable donations, in the trust.

Chapter 6: Preventing Family Drama: Keeping the Peace

How to Avoid Family Disputes Over Your Estate

When someone passes away, emotions are already running high. Grief, stress, and even guilt can affect decision-making, leading to family disputes over money, property, and inheritance. Many of these conflicts can be avoided with a solid estate plan and clear communication. Here's how to ensure your estate plan helps keep the peace among your loved ones:

1. Be Clear and Specific in Your Estate Plan

One of the biggest causes of family disputes is a lack of clarity in the estate plan. If your wishes are not clearly outlined, family members may interpret things differently, which can lead to disagreements. For instance, if your will simply states, "I leave my estate to my children," but doesn't specify how to divide the estate, it may lead to confusion about who gets what.

How to Avoid This:

- **Be specific** in your instructions about who gets what and when. Whether it's money, property, or sentimental items, clearly designate each item and the intended recipient.
- If you have **personal property** (like jewelry or heirlooms), be specific about who receives each item and ensure these instructions are included in your trust or will.
- If you want certain assets to go to charity or friends, ensure this is stated explicitly in the estate planning documents.

2. Use a Living Trust to Avoid Probate

Probate is the court process through which assets are distributed when someone dies. The process can be lengthy, costly, and public, which can lead to family disputes, especially if there are disagreements over the will or asset distribution. A will goes through probate, which means that your family's business is made public. This can sometimes stir up unnecessary conflict, especially if some beneficiaries feel they were treated unfairly.

How to Avoid This:

- By using a **living trust**, you can avoid the probate process entirely. Trusts allow for private distribution of assets, preventing public court hearings that can lead to arguments.
- When your estate avoids probate, your family members can begin the process of inheritance much sooner, reducing the stress of waiting for months or years to receive their share.
- A living trust also ensures that **everything** is distributed according to your wishes, leaving little room for interpretation or conflict.

3. Appoint a Neutral Trustee

When choosing someone to manage your estate, it's important to think about the person's ability to be impartial. Appointing a family member or close friend as a trustee may seem like a natural choice, but it can sometimes lead to conflicts, especially if the trustee is also a beneficiary. The situation becomes even more complicated if multiple family members are involved and there are competing interests.

How to Avoid This:

- **Appoint a neutral, third-party trustee** (such as a bank, trust company, or financial professional) who can manage your estate impartially. This can help ensure that your estate is handled professionally and that all beneficiaries are treated fairly.
- If you do choose a family member, consider choosing someone who has the skills to handle financial matters and who is emotionally stable enough to manage any family disputes that may arise.

4. Address Family Dynamics Early

Family dynamics can complicate estate planning, particularly when there are longstanding disputes, imbalances in wealth, or special family circumstances (such as one child being more involved in caregiving for aging parents). It's important to acknowledge these dynamics upfront and address them in your estate plan to prevent misunderstandings.

How to Avoid This:

- Have **honest conversations** with your family about your estate plan. Be transparent about who will receive what and why you've made those decisions.
- If you have children who are involved in caregiving or other special roles, consider allocating assets to recognize their contributions. This can help avoid resentment among siblings or other family members.
- If you are leaving a portion of your estate to a charity or a non-relative, explain why this decision was made to avoid family members feeling slighted or angry.

5. Create a Fair but Firm Plan

Estate planning is about creating fairness, but that doesn't mean every child or beneficiary gets an equal share. Sometimes, distributing assets equally doesn't reflect the needs or contributions of family members. For example, if one child has already received financial assistance during their lifetime, it may not be fair to divide assets equally among siblings. Similarly, if one child has been the primary caregiver for an aging parent, that child may deserve a larger share of the estate.

How to Avoid This:

- **Customize your plan** based on the needs of your beneficiaries. If one child is financially independent, they might not need as much as a child who is still struggling.
- Consider providing for **special needs children** or **caregivers** who have made sacrifices.
- The key is to ensure that the distribution reflects your family's individual circumstances, not just an equal split.

The 7 Deadly Mistakes That Sink Most Estate Plans

Even with the best of intentions, many estate plans fail due to common mistakes that can be easily avoided. Below are the **seven deadly mistakes** that can undermine your estate plan and lead to family disputes:

1. Failing to Update Your Plan Regularly

Life changes—children are born, spouses pass away, assets fluctuate, and personal relationships evolve. If you don't update your estate plan regularly to reflect these changes, it can cause confusion or result in outdated provisions. For instance, you may have named an ex-spouse as a beneficiary or trustee, but this designation no longer reflects your current wishes.

How to Avoid This:

- Regularly review your trust or will to ensure it reflects your current circumstances.
- Update your plan whenever there is a significant life change, such as marriage, divorce, the birth of children, or the acquisition of new property.

2. Overlooking Tax Implications

Many people fail to consider the potential tax consequences of their estate plan. This includes both **estate taxes** and **income taxes**. If you don't properly plan for these, your beneficiaries may end up losing a significant portion of their inheritance to taxes.

How to Avoid This:

- Consult with an estate planning attorney or tax advisor to understand the tax implications of your estate plan.
- Take advantage of strategies like gifting, charitable donations, and tax-efficient trust structures to reduce the tax burden on your beneficiaries.

3. Not Funding the Trust Properly

A trust is only effective if it is **funded**. This means that you need to legally transfer your assets into the trust, including real estate, bank accounts, investment accounts, and other valuables. Failing to fund the trust properly is one of the most common mistakes people make, and it can lead to assets being caught up in probate.

How to Avoid This:

- Make sure to **retitle assets** in the name of the trust.
- Regularly check to ensure that any new assets you acquire are properly transferred into the trust.

4. Not Naming a Successor Trustee

Failing to name a **successor trustee** can cause delays and confusion if the original trustee is unable to serve. If you don't appoint a successor, the court may need to appoint one, and this could lead to further delays in managing the trust.

How to Avoid This:

- Always name a **successor trustee** and a secondary successor trustee in case your first choice is unable or unwilling to serve.

5. Leaving Ambiguous Instructions

When instructions are vague or unclear, it opens the door for potential disagreements. For example, if you leave a portion of your estate to "my children" but do not specify how it should be divided, it may lead to confusion or disputes over how the assets should be distributed.

How to Avoid This:

- Be **specific** and clear about your wishes. Provide exact instructions for the distribution of assets and include details for each beneficiary.
- Avoid vague language like "to my family" or "for my children" unless it's followed by specific instructions.

6. Not Considering Digital Assets

In today's world, digital assets—such as email accounts, social media accounts, cryptocurrencies, and digital files—are often overlooked in estate planning. If you fail to plan for the distribution of these assets, your heirs may have difficulty accessing them.

How to Avoid This:

- Create a plan for your digital assets. Include passwords, accounts, and any instructions on how they should be handled.
- Consider appointing someone to handle your digital affairs if they need to be accessed after your death.

7. Ignoring Family Dynamics

Failing to consider family relationships and dynamics can lead to disputes. If you have children who have different financial needs or have been involved in caregiving, it may not be fair to divide your estate equally. Additionally, not acknowledging potential conflicts can create tension among your loved ones.

How to Avoid This:

- **Be fair** but also considerate of family dynamics. If certain family members have contributed more or have specific needs, take that into account when distributing assets.
- **Communicate openly** with your family about your intentions. This can help avoid misunderstandings and make the process easier on everyone.

Creating Family Harmony: Communicating Your Wishes

Clear communication is one of the most important tools in avoiding family disputes over your estate. Without clear communication, your family may be left in the dark about your intentions, leading to confusion, anger, or even legal challenges. Here are several strategies to ensure your wishes are understood and respected:

1. Have Open Conversations

Talking to your family members about your estate plan may feel uncomfortable, but it is necessary. Having a candid conversation with your heirs can help them understand why you made certain decisions, reducing the potential for disputes later. Explain your reasoning behind specific decisions, such as why you left more to one child or why certain assets are going to charity.

How to Communicate:

- Set up a time to meet with your family and explain the basics of your estate plan.
- Be open to their questions and concerns and try to address them respectfully.

2. Provide a Letter of Instruction

In addition to the formal legal documents, consider writing a **letter of instruction**. This is a personal letter where you can explain the details of your estate plan in a more informal way. It's a great opportunity to provide clarity on decisions that may seem unusual to your heirs and offer personal messages to each beneficiary.

How to Write a Letter of Instruction:

- Write a clear, heartfelt letter outlining your wishes.
- Address any concerns or questions you think your family members may have.

- Ensure the letter is updated periodically.

3. Ensure Your Plan Is Accessible

Make sure that your family knows where to find your estate planning documents. Whether it's a digital file or physical copies, ensure that your trusted loved ones or executors know how to access the documents when needed.

How to Share Your Plan:

- Keep your documents in a safe, secure location, such as a fireproof safe or a safe deposit box.
- Inform your family members of the location of these documents, or consider storing copies with a trusted attorney.

Addressing Potential Conflicts Before They Start

One of the most significant and often overlooked aspects of estate planning is the potential for family conflict. While the primary goal of creating a living trust or will is to ensure your assets are distributed according to your wishes, another critical goal is to minimize the chance of disputes arising among your loved ones once you're gone. These conflicts often arise due to misunderstandings, unclear instructions, or assumptions about what the deceased would have wanted.

By addressing potential conflicts proactively, you can reduce the likelihood of family members feeling hurt, neglected, or wronged. Creating a plan that not only distributes assets clearly but also addresses potential disputes and outlines expectations for your loved ones can go a long way in keeping the peace. The following section will delve into common sources of conflict and provide strategies for mitigating these issues before they arise.

1. Identifying Common Sources of Conflict

Before we discuss how to prevent conflicts, it's important to understand where the tensions and misunderstandings typically arise. Here are some of the most common sources of family conflict in estate planning:

1.1 Unequal Distribution of Assets

One of the most frequent causes of conflict among beneficiaries is when the estate is not divided equally. This can cause resentment, especially if one family member feels they are being treated unfairly. For example, if one child receives a larger portion of the estate due to their role as a caregiver or because of financial circumstances, other siblings might feel slighted.

1.2 Lack of Clarity in the Trust or Will

Vague or ambiguous language in your estate planning documents can leave room for misinterpretation. If the distribution of assets is not clearly defined, family members may argue about who gets what. This is particularly common when the instructions are open-ended or when specific family heirlooms or sentimental items are not designated.

1.3 Step-Parent and Blended Family Issues

Blended families often face unique challenges in estate planning. Children from previous marriages, stepchildren, and biological children may all have different expectations or desires about how assets should be distributed. Without clear instructions, this can lead to accusations of favoritism or neglect.

1.4 Personal or Emotional Attachments to Specific Assets

Sentimental value can cloud decision-making and create tension. Family members may have strong emotional connections to certain possessions, such as jewelry, artwork, or even a family home. If these assets are not specifically mentioned in the trust or will, it can lead to disputes about who should inherit these items.

1.5 Disagreements Over the Executor or Trustee

If family members disagree on who should manage the estate, it can cause significant delays and emotional turmoil. The person you designate as the executor or trustee is responsible for ensuring your wishes are followed, so appointing a trustworthy and competent individual is crucial.

1.6 Health Care and End-of-Life Decisions

Estate planning often involves decisions regarding your health care in the event you become incapacitated. If your loved ones don't know what you would want in these situations, it can lead to disagreements over life-sustaining treatment, funeral arrangements, or medical decisions.

2. How to Address Potential Conflicts Before They Start

The best way to prevent conflicts is to address them before they arise. Here are several steps you can take to proactively minimize misunderstandings and keep the peace among your beneficiaries.

2.1 Be Transparent About Your Wishes

One of the most effective ways to prevent conflicts is to ensure that your family members know exactly what to expect. Transparency is key. While the legal aspects of estate planning are important, **communicating your intentions clearly** to your loved ones can help avoid resentment or confusion down the road.

How to Be Transparent:

- **Discuss your estate plan with your beneficiaries**: Having an open conversation about your estate planning decisions can help family members understand your reasoning. If you've made unequal distributions based on specific circumstances, explain why. If you've chosen one child to be your executor due to their financial acumen or organizational skills, make sure everyone knows why this choice was made.
- **Write a Letter of Instruction**: In addition to your legal documents, consider writing a letter that explains your estate plan in detail. This can help clarify decisions that may be questioned later. For example, you can explain why you decided to leave the family home to one child, or why you chose to donate part of your estate to charity.
- **Hold a Family Meeting**: If you feel comfortable, arrange a family meeting to discuss your estate planning choices. It's an opportunity for everyone to ask questions, express concerns, and better understand your intentions. This may prevent misunderstandings later on and can be particularly helpful for blended families or those with complicated dynamics.

2.2 Be Specific in Your Estate Planning Documents

The more precise you are in your trust or will, the less room there is for interpretation. Vague or general language can lead to confusion and disagreements. It's essential to include specific instructions for both the distribution of your assets and the management of your estate.

How to Be Specific:

- **Clearly Define Asset Distribution**: Instead of saying "I leave everything to my children," specify who gets what, and if necessary, provide reasoning for your decisions. For example, "I leave my jewelry collection to my daughter, [Name], because she has always had a passion for these items."
- **Be Explicit About Sentimental Items**: If there are specific items that hold sentimental value, make sure to designate them clearly in your estate planning documents. If you're leaving the family home to one child, outline why that decision was made. Consider creating a separate **memorandum** listing personal items and their intended recipients.
- **Clarify Trustee and Executor Responsibilities**: The roles of your executor or trustee should be explicitly outlined. If you're appointing a family member, make sure they understand the responsibilities and have the legal authority to make decisions on behalf of the estate.

2.3 Plan for Equal or Fair Distribution

When distributing your assets, **equality** doesn't always mean fairness. Some family members may need more financial support than others. For example, if one child has been a caregiver or has struggled financially, you may choose to give them a larger share of your estate. However, this decision should be communicated clearly to avoid the perception of favoritism.

How to Plan for Fair Distribution:

- **Fairness vs. Equality**: If you're choosing to give more to one beneficiary due to their needs or contributions, explain this decision clearly in your will or trust. For example, "I leave a larger portion of my estate to my daughter, [Name], because she has provided long-term care for me and contributed more time and energy to my well-being than my other children."

- **Provide Equal Value, Not Necessarily Equal Amounts**: If there is a dispute about the distribution, consider offering each beneficiary assets of equal value, even if the quantity isn't equal. For instance, one child may receive a valuable family heirloom, while another child may receive a cash sum that is equivalent in value.

2.4 Choose a Neutral Executor or Trustee

Choosing the right **executor** (for a will) or **trustee** (for a trust) is one of the most important decisions in estate planning. This person will be responsible for carrying out your wishes and ensuring your assets are distributed according to your plan. If the wrong person is chosen, it can lead to conflicts or delays.

How to Choose the Right Executor/Trustee:

- **Consider Neutral Third Parties**: If you anticipate that family members will have disputes over the executor or trustee, consider appointing a neutral third party, such as a trusted financial advisor, attorney, or even a bank or trust company, to manage the estate. This can help avoid conflicts of interest.
- **Ensure Competence and Trustworthiness**: The executor or trustee should have the ability to manage finances, make decisions, and handle potential disputes. If you choose a family member, make sure they are able to act impartially and maintain professionalism throughout the process.

2.5 Set Clear Expectations for Your Caregiving Wishes

In families where one member has taken on the role of caregiver, it is important to ensure that they are fairly compensated for their time and effort, if applicable, and that their contributions are acknowledged in your estate plan. Caregiving can take a significant emotional and physical toll, and it's essential to recognize this in your estate planning documents to prevent feelings of resentment.

How to Address Caregiving Contributions:

- **Provide for the Caregiver**: If one family member has been particularly involved in caregiving, consider providing them with a larger share of your estate, or make specific provisions for their care in the future.
- **Incorporate Caregiving in Your Will or Trust**: Address caregiving contributions directly in your estate planning documents by explaining your reasoning for giving a larger share to the caregiver, or by acknowledging their efforts in a letter of instruction.

How to Handle "That's Not What They Would Have Wanted"

At some point during the estate settlement process, you may hear your beneficiaries say, "That's not what they would have wanted." This is a common phrase used when a family member disagrees with the terms of a will or trust. While it's natural for beneficiaries to be upset, especially if they didn't get what they expected, it's important to handle this situation carefully to avoid unnecessary conflict.

1. Anticipate Potential Disagreements

Before you even pass away, it's important to anticipate where disputes might arise and address those areas directly. As we discussed earlier, being specific in your distribution clauses can prevent disagreements. But beyond the technical aspects of the estate plan, consider the emotional attachments your family may have to certain assets. Communicate openly about potential sources of conflict and explain why you made certain decisions.

2. Provide an Explanation in Writing

If family members raise concerns about the estate plan after you're gone, having a clear explanation in writing can help alleviate misunderstandings. This is where a **Letter of Instruction** can be invaluable. This letter allows you to provide context for your decisions, offering insight into your thought process and reasoning behind specific bequests.

3. Consider the Use of Mediation

If family members continue to disagree after your passing, consider using a **mediator**. Mediation can help resolve disputes without the need for expensive and emotionally draining litigation. A mediator can guide your family through the process of resolving conflicts and reaching a compromise, ensuring that your wishes are respected while keeping family relationships intact.

4. Keep Calm and Firmly Stand by Your Wishes

Estate planning is a deeply personal process. You are the one who knows what you want, what you value, and what you intend for your family's future. If your estate plan was thoughtfully created and clearly communicated, you should feel confident that you made the right decisions. In situations where beneficiaries question your wishes, gently remind them that you have made your decisions with their best interests in mind, and encourage them to respect your choices.

Chapter 7: Incapacity Planning: What Happens If You Can't Act?

Why You Need an Incapacity Plan

None of us can predict the future, and there's always the possibility that at some point, we may become unable to manage our own affairs. This could happen due to an unexpected accident, a sudden illness, or a gradual decline in mental or physical health. **Incapacity** is a state in which a person is no longer able to make decisions for themselves, whether due to a mental or physical impairment. Without an incapacity plan, your loved ones could face considerable challenges in taking care of you or managing your financial and personal matters.

The Importance of Incapacity Planning

1. **Avoiding Court Intervention**
   Without an incapacity plan, a family member may need to petition a court to appoint a **guardian** or **conservator** to manage your affairs. This process can be time-consuming, expensive, and emotionally taxing. An incapacity plan can bypass this process by appointing someone in advance to take over if needed, making sure your wishes are respected and your affairs are handled smoothly.
2. **Preventing Family Conflict**
   In situations where incapacity is involved, family members may have differing opinions on how to handle your care or manage your assets. Having a clear incapacity plan that designates a **trusted individual** (such as a power of attorney) can avoid conflicts or confusion, ensuring that there's no ambiguity about who is in charge.
3. **Maintaining Control Over Your Health and Finances**

While you may not be able to make decisions for yourself if you become incapacitated, an incapacity plan ensures that those decisions are made by someone you trust. It allows you to maintain control over your affairs even when you're no longer able to handle them yourself.

1. **Peace of Mind for Loved Ones**

> Having an incapacity plan in place provides peace of mind for your family members. They'll know exactly who is responsible for making decisions on your behalf, and there won't be uncertainty about what you would have wanted.

Incapacity planning is not just for the elderly; it is for everyone, regardless of age. Accidents, illnesses, or unexpected medical conditions can affect anyone at any time. By creating an incapacity plan, you are preparing for the unexpected, ensuring that your wishes are respected and that your loved ones are able to act on your behalf if the need arises.

Power of Attorney: What It Is and Why It's Crucial

One of the most important tools in incapacity planning is the **Power of Attorney (POA)**. This legal document allows you to designate someone (called your "**agent**" or "**attorney-in-fact**") to act on your behalf in the event that you are unable to make decisions for yourself.

What Is a Power of Attorney?

A **Power of Attorney** is a legal document that grants another person the authority to act on your behalf in legal, financial, and health-related matters. The scope of authority granted can vary depending on the type of POA you create. There are different types of powers of attorney, each designed for specific purposes. These documents are critical in incapacity planning, as they allow someone you trust to handle matters on your behalf when you cannot.

There are two main types of **Power of Attorney**:

1. **General Power of Attorney**
   A **General Power of Attorney** gives the agent broad authority to act on your behalf. This may include managing your finances, signing contracts, handling your business affairs, and making other day-to-day decisions. It is often used in situations where you are temporarily unavailable, such as being out of the country or incapacitated.

Key points:

- The agent has broad authority, and can manage most aspects of your financial and legal affairs.
- This type of POA may become invalid if you become incapacitated (unless specified otherwise in the document).

1. **Durable Power of Attorney**

A **Durable Power of Attorney** remains in effect if you become incapacitated. This is an essential tool for incapacity planning. It allows your agent to manage your affairs even if you are mentally or physically incapable of doing so yourself. Without a durable POA, your family may need to go to court to obtain guardianship or conservatorship, a lengthy and expensive process.

Key points:

- The agent's authority continues if you become incapacitated.
- It's often used for long-term or permanent incapacity, such as a serious illness, accident, or dementia.

1. **Limited Power of Attorney**

A **Limited Power of Attorney** is more specific in scope and grants the agent authority only to act in particular situations or for particular tasks. For example, you might give a limited POA to someone to handle a single transaction, like selling a piece of property.

Key points:

- The authority granted is very specific and limited to certain actions.
- It expires once the specified task or time period is completed.

Why a Power of Attorney is Crucial for Incapacity Planning

1. **Financial and Legal Decision-Making**

If you become incapacitated, someone will need to manage your financial matters, such as paying bills, managing investments, or handling taxes. A **Durable Power of Attorney** ensures that someone you trust can step in and make these decisions for you. Without it, your family may have to go through a lengthy legal process to gain control over your finances.

1. **Health Care Decisions**

A Medical Power of Attorney (also known as a **health care proxy**) authorizes the agent to make health-care choices on your behalf if you are unable to communicate your desires. This may involve decisions about medical treatment, life support, and end-of-life care.

1. **Minimizing Delays**

A Power of Attorney allows your agent to act immediately when you become incapacitated, avoiding the need for your family to go to court for guardianship. This minimizes delays and ensures that important decisions are made quickly and efficiently.

1. **Avoiding Family Disputes**

By naming a trusted agent in advance, you reduce the likelihood of conflicts among family members. Without a POA, there could be disagreements over who should make decisions on your behalf, which could lead to legal battles and emotional stress.

Healthcare Directives and End-of-Life Decisions

Along with the **Power of Attorney**, another essential component of incapacity planning is the **health care directive**, sometimes called a **living will.** This document allows you to express your preferences for medical treatment in the event that you are unable to communicate these wishes yourself.

What Is a Healthcare Directive?

A **healthcare directive** is a legal document that outlines your preferences for medical treatment if you become incapacitated. It can include instructions regarding life-sustaining treatment, organ donation, and end-of-life care. A healthcare directive is critical in ensuring that your wishes are respected when it comes to critical medical decisions.

There are two key components of healthcare directives:

1. **Living Will**

A **living will** is a written statement that details your preferences for medical care if you are in a terminal condition or permanently unconscious. It typically includes instructions regarding:

- **Life support**: Whether you want to be placed on life support or not.
- **Organ donation**: Whether you wish to donate your organs after death.
- **End-of-life care**: Whether you want to receive palliative care to ease pain and suffering, even if it may hasten your death.

1. **Healthcare Power of Attorney**

A **healthcare power of attorney** (also known as a **healthcare proxy**) designates a person to make medical decisions on your behalf if you are unable to make them yourself. Unlike a living will, which provides instructions on medical treatment, a healthcare power of attorney grants authority to a trusted person to make decisions based on your preferences when they arise.

Why Healthcare Directives Are Crucial

1. **Ensuring Your Wishes Are Followed**

A healthcare directive ensures that medical providers and your family understand and follow your wishes regarding your health care. Without this document, your family may be left to make difficult decisions without knowing your preferences, leading to stress and potential conflict.

1. **Avoiding Family Disputes**

Healthcare decisions, particularly those involving life support or end-of-life care, can create serious conflict among family members. Some may want to prolong your life at all costs, while others may prefer to allow nature to take its course. By specifying your wishes in advance, you eliminate the potential for disputes and ensure that your family does not have to make these decisions on your behalf.

1. **Reducing Emotional Stress**

Healthcare directives help reduce the emotional burden on your family members. They provide clear guidance during an emotionally charged time, which can ease the decision-making process and help family members focus on supporting each other rather than debating what you would have wanted.

1. **Ensuring Your Dignity**

By outlining your preferences for medical care, you maintain control over your end-of-life care, ensuring that your dignity is preserved even if you cannot communicate your wishes. A healthcare directive empowers you to make decisions about how you want to be treated and under what circumstances.

Key Decisions Covered by Healthcare Directives

1. **Life Support**

If you become terminally ill or permanently unconscious, you can specify whether you want life-sustaining treatments, such as a ventilator or feeding tube, to be used. This allows you to make decisions about how long you want to be kept alive artificially.

1. **Organ Donation**

Healthcare directives often include instructions about organ donation. You can indicate whether you want your organs donated upon death, and this can ensure that your organs go to those who need them, if you wish to contribute in this way.

1. **Palliative Care**

For those with terminal illnesses, a healthcare directive can specify your preferences for **palliative care**, which focuses on providing relief from symptoms and pain rather than curing the illness. This can include hospice care, which provides comfort and emotional support to patients and their families in the final stages of life.

1. **Autopsy**

You can specify whether or not you would like an autopsy performed after your death. This is an important consideration for some families, particularly if they have religious or cultural preferences regarding post-mortem examinations.

Guardianship for Minor Children: Planning for Their Future

Who Steps In When You Can't Act and What Authority They Have

The appointment of a guardian is a critical part of any parent's estate plan, and it's essential to understand who can step in when you are unable to care for your children, as well as the authority they will have. Guardianship laws can vary from state to state, but the general concept remains the same: a guardian is someone who assumes legal responsibility for a child when their biological parents are unable to care for them.

What Is Guardianship?

Guardianship is a legal relationship in which a person (the **guardian**) is given the authority to care for a child (the **ward**) and make decisions on their behalf. This legal relationship can arise under several circumstances, including the death of a parent, the incapacity of a parent, or if the parents are temporarily unable to care for the child.

The guardian has many responsibilities, such as:

1. **Providing Physical Care**: The guardian is responsible for meeting the child's physical needs, including housing, food, and clothing.
2. **Making Educational Decisions**: The guardian makes decisions about the child's education, including where they go to school and what type of education they receive.
3. **Making Medical Decisions**: The guardian has the authority to make healthcare decisions for the child, including medical treatments and therapies.
4. **Managing Financial Assets**: If the child inherits assets, the guardian may also have the responsibility to manage and use the funds in the child's best interest.

The **authority** granted to a guardian will depend on the legal framework in place. In some cases, a guardian may have full authority to make all decisions regarding the child's well-being, while in other situations, the court may impose restrictions or appoint additional individuals to assist in decision-making.

Who Can Be a Guardian?

The **guardian** can be any person whom the parents trust to care for their children in the event of their death or incapacity. Typically, parents choose a family member, such as a grandparent, aunt, or uncle, but they may also designate a close family friend or even a professional guardian, if desired.

When selecting a guardian, consider the following:

- **Relationship with the Child**: Ideally, the guardian should have a close and positive relationship with the child. It is important that the child feels comfortable and safe with the guardian.
- **Values and Parenting Style**: The guardian should share similar values and parenting styles, especially when it comes to issues like discipline, education, and healthcare.
- **Financial Stability**: While guardians do not need to be wealthy, it is essential that they are financially stable enough to provide for the child's needs without undue strain.
- **Physical and Emotional Capability**: The guardian should be in good health and have the emotional and physical stamina to care for a child, especially if the child has special needs or requires extra attention.
- **Willingness to Serve**: It is essential that the person you choose as a guardian is willing to accept the responsibility. Discussing this decision with them beforehand ensures they understand the commitment and are prepared to take on this role.

What Type of Guardianship Exists?

There are different types of guardianships, depending on the child's needs and the specifics of your estate plan. These include:

1. **Legal Guardianship**: A legal guardian has full legal custody of the child and is responsible for all decisions related to the child's care,

health, education, and finances. This is the most common form of guardianship when a parent dies or becomes incapacitated.

2. **Temporary Guardianship**: In some cases, a temporary guardian may be appointed to care for the child in the short term. This often occurs when parents are unavailable for a period (due to hospitalization, travel, or another reason) but plan to resume parental duties once they are able. Temporary guardianship usually lasts a set period of time and is typically less formal than legal guardianship.
3. **Standby Guardianship**: A standby guardian is someone designated to step in as the child's guardian in the event of a parent's incapacity or death. This is typically established in a **power of attorney** or a **healthcare directive**, where a parent appoints a standby guardian to assume guardianship if the parent becomes incapacitated or dies. This type of guardianship is useful for parents who are elderly, ill, or otherwise expect a potential incapacity but are not yet unable to care for their children.

What Authority Does a Guardian Have?

Once a guardian is appointed, they have the authority to make decisions regarding the child's physical and emotional well-being. The extent of this authority depends on the type of guardianship established, but the general powers of a guardian are:

1. **Physical Custody**: The guardian has the right to provide a home and physical care for the child, ensuring that the child has their basic needs met.
2. **Educational Decisions**: Guardians are responsible for making decisions regarding the child's education, including choosing schools, overseeing academic progress, and addressing special educational needs.
3. **Medical Decisions**: The guardian has the authority to make healthcare decisions, including choosing medical providers, approving treatments, and making decisions about the child's health, especially in emergencies.

4. **Financial Management**: If the child inherits assets, the guardian may be responsible for managing the child's financial interests until the child reaches adulthood. The guardian must act in the best interest of the child, managing the assets prudently and providing for the child's needs.
5. **Access to Legal Authority**: If necessary, the guardian can represent the child in legal matters, such as dealing with lawsuits, entering into contracts on the child's behalf, and addressing the child's legal needs.

How to Ensure Guardianship is Legally Established

To ensure that the guardian you've chosen has the authority to step in and care for your children, you must **legally establish guardianship** in your estate plan. This involves making it official through the proper legal channels and ensuring that the guardian has the authority to make decisions on behalf of your children if you are unable to do so.

Here are the steps you should take:

1. Designate a Guardian in Your Will or Trust

The first step in legally establishing guardianship for your children is to include a **guardian designation** in your will or living trust. This document should clearly state who will care for your children if you pass away or become incapacitated.

- If you have a **will**, include a guardianship clause naming your preferred guardian(s) and outlining any special instructions.
- If you have a **living trust**, this clause can be included within the trust document. The benefit of naming a guardian in a living trust is that it can be handled privately, without court involvement, whereas a will generally requires probate.

Make sure that your guardian choice is in writing and signed according to the laws in your state. This makes your wishes legally binding and can help prevent disputes among family members.

2. Discuss the Decision with the Guardian

Before naming someone as your child's guardian, have a candid discussion with them to ensure they are willing to take on the responsibility. The role of a guardian is significant, and the individual you choose should be fully aware of what it entails. Talk about your children's care, your expectations, and any issues they should be aware of (such as medical needs, religious preferences, or schooling).

3. Consider a Backup Guardian

It's important to designate an **alternate guardian** in case your first choice is unable to serve. This could happen if the first choice is unable to take on the responsibility, moves away, or passes away. Having a second option ensures that there is no uncertainty if your primary guardian cannot step in.

4. Formalize the Guardianship Through the Court (if Necessary)

While a will or trust allows you to designate a guardian, in some cases, you may need to go through the **court process** to formalize the guardianship. This is typically necessary if there is a dispute about who should be the guardian or if the court needs to approve your choice. However, if your will or trust clearly names a guardian and there is no challenge, the court usually honors that designation.

Guardianship and Financial Responsibility

If the guardian will also manage your child's inheritance or assets, you may need to set up specific guidelines for managing the child's finances. In many cases, the guardian will also be the **conservator** of the child's financial assets, and this role requires a fiduciary duty to manage the child's inheritance responsibly. It's important to include clear instructions on how the guardian should manage and distribute these assets.

Chapter 8: Trust Taxes and Common Myths

What a Living Trust Does Not Do for Taxes

Living trusts are incredibly useful tools for estate planning, but it's important to understand that they do not provide **automatic tax benefits**. There are several myths about living trusts and taxes, and it's easy to see why people may believe a living trust can help them avoid taxes. However, it's critical to recognize what a living trust **does not** do for taxes.

1. A Living Trust Does Not Avoid Estate Taxes

One of the most common myths is that a living trust will help you avoid **estate taxes**. This is false. A living trust does not automatically shield your estate from federal estate taxes, which are applied to the value of your estate when you die.

Why It's a Myth:

Estate taxes are based on the value of the assets you own at the time of your death, and **a living trust does not remove assets from your estate**. If you transfer assets into your trust, they are still considered part of your taxable estate. The government will still assess estate taxes on the total value of your estate, whether the assets are in your personal name or in the trust.

- **Federal Estate Tax Threshold**: As of the current federal laws, estate taxes are applied to estates worth over $11.7 million (this threshold can change due to new legislation). For estates worth more than this amount, estate taxes may be applicable, regardless of whether the assets are held in a trust.

2. A Living Trust Does Not Reduce Income Taxes

Another misconception is that a living trust helps reduce **income taxes**. While a living trust can be structured to manage your assets efficiently, it does not inherently lower your income tax liability.

Why It's a Myth:

A living trust is considered a **grantor trust**, meaning that the grantor (the person who creates the trust) is still treated as the owner of the assets for income tax purposes. All income generated by the trust's assets, such as dividends, interest, and capital gains, is reported on the grantor's personal income tax return.

This means that the income generated by the assets in the living trust is taxed at the grantor's **personal income tax rate**, just as if the assets were still in their name. In other words, a living trust does not provide any special tax break for income taxes.

3. A Living Trust Does Not Shield You from Gift Taxes

Many people think that transferring assets into a living trust is a way to avoid **gift taxes**. This is not the case. When you transfer assets into a living trust, you are essentially gifting those assets to the trust, which can trigger gift taxes if the transfer exceeds the annual exemption limit.

Why It's a Myth:

The **gift tax** applies to the transfer of assets that are given away without receiving something of equal value in return. While you are still alive and the living trust is revocable (meaning you can change the terms or take assets out of it), the transfer of assets does not trigger gift taxes. However, once assets are placed in the trust, if you make irrevocable gifts or leave assets to beneficiaries, the gift tax rules apply.

- **Gift Tax Exemption**: For 2021, the annual gift tax exclusion is $15,000 per individual. If you transfer more than this amount to a beneficiary or into a trust, you may be required to file a gift tax return and pay taxes, depending on the value of the transfer.

4. A Living Trust Does Not Avoid Generation-Skipping Transfer Taxes

Some people believe that a living trust can help them avoid **generation-skipping transfer (GST) taxes**, which are taxes applied when assets skip a generation and are transferred directly to grandchildren or more remote descendants. However, a living trust does not provide any special protection from these taxes.

Why It's a Myth:

Generation-skipping transfer taxes are designed to ensure that wealth does not pass from one generation to another without taxation. If assets are transferred to grandchildren or great-grandchildren directly, GST taxes could apply, and a living trust doesn't automatically exempt you from this.

To avoid generation-skipping taxes, a more specialized estate planning tool, such as a **generation-skipping trust**, may be needed.

How Living Trusts Affect Your Tax Planning

While living trusts don't shield you from taxes, they do have an impact on how your assets are handled for tax purposes. Here's how a living trust plays a role in tax planning:

1. Trusts and Estate Tax Planning

One of the primary reasons people create living trusts is to streamline the estate planning process and avoid probate. However, when it comes to **estate taxes**, a living trust doesn't reduce the taxable value of your estate. What a living trust can do, though, is ensure a **smoother transfer** of your assets upon death, which can reduce the time and costs associated with probate.

A trust can also be an essential part of a **tax strategy** to minimize estate taxes. For high-net-worth individuals, **Irrevocable Trusts**, rather than a revocable living trust, can be a better option for estate tax planning because they remove assets from your estate entirely. This can be particularly important if your estate exceeds the estate tax exemption threshold.

- **Taxable Estate**: The value of your estate includes everything you own (real estate, investments, savings, etc.), and it is taxed after your death. Using an irrevocable trust or other tax-efficient strategies, you can potentially reduce the size of your taxable estate.

2. Trusts and Income Tax Filing

As mentioned earlier, a living trust is a **grantor trust** for tax purposes, meaning the grantor is responsible for paying income taxes on the assets held in the trust. For this reason, **income generated by the trust** (such as dividends or interest) is reported on the grantor's personal tax return.

Tax Filing Implications:

- A **revocable living trust** does not require a separate tax identification number (TIN). Instead, the **grantor's Social Security number** is used for the trust's income tax filings.
- If the grantor becomes incapacitated or passes away, the successor

trustee will manage the assets, but the income generated from those assets will still be taxed as part of the estate's tax filings until the assets are distributed to beneficiaries.

This means that, although a living trust provides many benefits, it does not provide any tax relief when it comes to income taxes. However, one of the advantages of a living trust is that it allows for **seamless continuity** in tax reporting, making the transition smoother for your family and beneficiaries.

3. Avoiding Probate and Its Associated Costs

One of the main benefits of a living trust is that it allows your estate to **bypass probate**. Probate can be expensive and time-consuming, and while it doesn't directly affect your tax liability, it does affect your **overall estate administration costs**.

When an estate goes through probate, the court fees, legal fees, and other administrative costs can quickly add up. These fees may be deducted from your estate before distribution to your heirs, which could reduce the amount they inherit.

While probate does not directly affect the estate's **income tax** liabilities, avoiding probate through a living trust can reduce the **costs** associated with settling the estate, and thus increase the value of the inheritance passed on to beneficiaries. These savings, in turn, help beneficiaries preserve more of their wealth.

Trust Taxes: What You Need to Know

Understanding trust taxes is essential when it comes to ensuring your estate plan works as you intended. A living trust, like other types of trusts, has specific tax rules that govern how it is taxed during the grantor's lifetime and after death.

1. Taxes on Trust Income

During the life of the trust, the income generated by the assets within the trust is taxed to the **grantor**. However, once the grantor passes away, the **trust itself becomes a separate taxable entity**. This means that the trust may need to file its own tax returns and pay taxes on income generated from the assets in the trust.

- **Grantor Trusts**: In a **revocable living trust**, the income generated by the assets remains taxable to the grantor during their lifetime. This means you will report the income on your personal tax return, and the trust doesn't pay taxes separately. When you die, the trust becomes irrevocable and can no longer be modified or revoked.
- **Non-Grantor Trusts**: After the grantor's death, the trust becomes a **non-grantor trust**. Non-grantor trusts are separate taxable entities and must file their own tax returns. Trusts are taxed at higher rates than individuals, so the income generated by the trust can be subject to significant taxes if it's not distributed to the beneficiaries.

2. Estate Tax Implications of Living Trusts

As mentioned earlier, **estate taxes** apply to the total value of your estate after you die. A living trust does not automatically reduce estate taxes, but it can help your beneficiaries avoid probate, which can be costly and time-consuming. If your estate is large enough to exceed the estate tax exemption, there are strategies you can use to minimize taxes, such as creating an **irrevocable trust** or making **annual gifts** to reduce the estate's taxable value.

- **Estate Tax Exemption**: The **estate tax exemption** determines how much of your estate is exempt from taxes. For 2021, the exemption is $11.7 million. Anything above that amount is taxed at federal estate tax rates, which can be as high as 40%. A living trust does not remove assets from your estate for tax purposes, but it helps ensure a smoother distribution process and can save your family time and money by avoiding probate.

3. Trusts and Capital Gains Taxes

If the assets held in a trust increase in value (such as stocks, real estate, or other investments), the sale or transfer of those assets could result in **capital gains taxes.** When the grantor transfers assets to the trust, it's important to understand the potential capital gains implications.

- **Step-Up in Basis**: One of the advantages of holding assets in a trust is that upon the grantor's death, the trust may benefit from a **step-up in basis** for assets such as real estate or stocks. This means that the **cost basis** of the asset is adjusted to its market value at the time of death, reducing the potential capital gains tax liability when the asset is sold.

How to Minimize Taxes Through Effective Planning

There are several strategies available to minimize taxes, whether it's income taxes during your lifetime, estate taxes at the time of your death, or gift taxes when transferring assets to your loved ones. Below are some of the most effective ways to reduce your tax burden and preserve your estate.

1. Utilize the Estate Tax Exemption

One of the most important ways to minimize estate taxes is to make full use of the **estate tax exemption**. The estate tax exemption determines how much of your estate can pass to your heirs without being subject to federal estate tax. As of 2021, the federal estate tax exemption is $11.7 million, meaning that you can leave up to this amount to your heirs without incurring estate taxes.

Strategies to Minimize Estate Taxes:

- **Lifetime Gifting**: You can take advantage of the **annual gift tax exclusion** (which is $15,000 per person per year in 2021) to transfer wealth to your heirs during your lifetime. By making annual gifts, you can reduce the size of your taxable estate while taking full advantage of the estate tax exemption.
- **Marital Deduction**: If you're married, you can use the **marital deduction**, which allows you to transfer assets to your spouse without incurring estate taxes. By leaving assets to your spouse, you effectively defer estate taxes until the second spouse passes away. This strategy is particularly useful if your estate exceeds the exemption limit.
- **Portability**: The **portability** rule allows a surviving spouse to use the estate tax exemption of their deceased spouse. If the first spouse dies without using their full estate tax exemption, the surviving spouse can take advantage of the unused portion. This can effectively double the amount that can pass tax-free.

2. Establish an Irrevocable Trust

One of the most effective ways to reduce estate taxes is to transfer assets into an **irrevocable trust**. When you transfer assets into an irrevocable trust, those assets are no longer considered part of your taxable estate. This reduces the overall value of your estate, which can lower your estate tax liability.

- **Irrevocable Life Insurance Trust (ILIT)**: One common type of irrevocable trust is the **ILIT**, which removes life insurance proceeds from your taxable estate. By placing life insurance policies into an ILIT, the death benefits will not be subject to estate taxes. This strategy is especially useful for high-net-worth individuals who want to pass on substantial life insurance benefits without triggering a tax burden.
- **Charitable Trusts**: Charitable remainder trusts (CRT) and charitable lead trusts (CLT) allow you to reduce the taxable value of your estate by donating assets to charity. These trusts also provide you with a charitable deduction, which can help reduce income taxes and estate taxes. If you want to leave a legacy to charity while benefiting from tax savings, these trusts are an excellent option.

3. Take Advantage of Gift and GST Tax Exemptions

While the **estate tax exemption** is important, the **gift tax exemption** allows you to transfer assets to heirs during your lifetime without triggering taxes. In addition to the annual gift exclusion, the **lifetime gift tax exemption** allows you to transfer up to $11.7 million (2021 figure) in assets without incurring gift taxes.

- **Use of Gift Tax Exemption**: If you have a large estate, using your **lifetime gift tax exemption** can help reduce the size of your taxable estate. By transferring assets to your heirs while you are alive, you can lower the overall value of your estate, potentially reducing estate taxes after your death.
- **Generation-Skipping Trust (GST)**: A **generation-skipping trust**

allows you to make gifts to grandchildren or other beneficiaries who are two or more generations below you. This helps avoid the **generation-skipping transfer tax**, which is a separate tax on large gifts made to people two generations or more younger than you. By using this type of trust, you can pass on wealth to younger generations without incurring additional taxes.

4. Minimize Capital Gains Taxes

While capital gains taxes are typically a concern for **income-producing assets**, they can also impact the distribution of assets from your estate. If your heirs inherit assets that have appreciated in value (e.g., real estate or stocks), they may be required to pay **capital gains taxes** when they sell those assets.

However, there is a **benefit of the step-up in basis** for inherited assets, which helps minimize capital gains taxes. When your heirs inherit assets like real estate or stocks, the **cost basis** (the value used to calculate capital gains tax) is adjusted to the **fair market value** at the time of your death. This means that any gains that occurred during your lifetime are effectively erased, and your heirs only pay capital gains taxes on any future appreciation.

How to Minimize Capital Gains Taxes:

- **Hold Assets Until Death**: Holding appreciated assets until your death and passing them on to your heirs can eliminate much of the capital gains tax burden. The step-up in basis means your heirs won't have to pay taxes on the gains that accrued during your lifetime.
- **Donate Appreciated Assets**: If you're charitable-minded, donating appreciated assets directly to charity (instead of selling them first) allows you to avoid capital gains taxes on the appreciation. Charitable contributions may also provide you with a charitable deduction for income tax purposes.

5. Use Tax-Advantaged Accounts and Investments

Certain types of investments and accounts offer tax advantages that can help minimize taxes, both during your lifetime and after your death.

- **Retirement Accounts**: Contributions to retirement accounts like **IRAs** and **401(k)s** are tax-deferred, meaning you don't pay taxes on the money you contribute until you withdraw it. However, these funds may be subject to estate taxes, so consider designating beneficiaries who will inherit the funds without triggering additional taxes.
- **529 College Savings Plans**: Contributions to 529 plans are not tax-deductible on the federal level, but the earnings grow tax-free, and distributions used for qualified educational expenses are also tax-free. This can be an effective way to transfer wealth to the next generation while minimizing taxes.

Common Tax Mistakes to Avoid

While estate planning offers many opportunities to minimize taxes, there are common tax mistakes that people often make. These mistakes can result in significant tax liabilities, delays in estate administration, and unnecessary costs for your beneficiaries. Below are the most common mistakes to watch out for when planning your estate:

1. Failing to Fund Your Trust Properly

One of the most significant mistakes people make is failing to **fund their trust**. A living trust must be funded for it to be effective in avoiding probate and reducing estate taxes. If assets are not transferred into the trust, they will be subject to probate, and the potential tax benefits of the trust will be lost.

How to Avoid This Mistake:

- Ensure that all of your assets are properly transferred into the trust. This includes real estate, bank accounts, investments, life insurance policies, and personal property.
- Regularly review your trust to ensure any new assets are also transferred into it.

2. Ignoring Gift and Estate Tax Exemption Limits

Failing to use the **gift and estate tax exemptions** effectively can result in a larger estate that is subject to unnecessary taxes. If you do not use your lifetime gift exemption, you may miss an opportunity to reduce the value of your estate and lower the potential estate tax liability.

How to Avoid This Mistake:

- Take advantage of annual gift exclusions and lifetime gift exemptions to transfer wealth to your heirs while you're alive.
- Make strategic gifts to your beneficiaries, particularly if your estate is near or above the exemption threshold.

3. Not Considering the Impact of State Taxes

In addition to federal estate taxes, many states impose their own estate or inheritance taxes. These state taxes can vary significantly, and it's important to be aware of the laws in your state of residence.

How to Avoid This Mistake:

- Research the estate tax laws in your state. If your state has a **state estate tax**, you may want to take additional steps to reduce the value of your taxable estate, such as making gifts or transferring assets to a trust.

4. Overlooking the Impact of Retirement Accounts

While **retirement accounts** like IRAs and 401(k)s offer tax-deferred growth, they can also result in significant tax liabilities for your heirs. Retirement accounts are taxed as **income** when the beneficiary withdraws the funds, and the funds may be subject to estate taxes as well.

How to Avoid This Mistake:

- Designate beneficiaries for your retirement accounts and be mindful of the potential tax implications for those beneficiaries.
- Consider converting some of your retirement accounts to **Roth IRAs**, which allow for tax-free withdrawals (though taxes are paid at the time of conversion).

Chapter 9: The DIY Danger: Why Template Trusts May Fail

The Risks of Using DIY Living Trust Templates

The idea of creating a living trust on your own using a pre-drafted template can seem attractive because it appears to save money on legal fees and offers convenience. However, the risks involved often outweigh the perceived benefits. When you use a template trust, you are relying on a one-size-fits-all document that may not be tailored to your specific needs, state laws, or personal situation. Here are the primary risks associated with DIY living trust templates:

1. Lack of Personalization and Tailoring

One of the most significant dangers of using a DIY living trust template is the **lack of personalization.** A generic template is written to apply to a broad audience, not considering the unique needs and complexities of your estate. For example, templates may not account for your specific wishes regarding how your assets should be distributed, or they may overlook important family dynamics (such as blended families or complex financial situations).

When using a template, you may not be able to fully address your situation in a way that makes sense for your estate plan. The document might not include all of the necessary provisions that are specific to your circumstances, leading to confusion, misinterpretation, or disputes later on.

For example:

- **Asset-specific issues**: If you own a business, a unique investment portfolio, or have special assets (e.g., art, family heirlooms, or digital assets), a generic trust template may not cover how those assets should be handled.
- **Family dynamics**: Blended families, estranged relationships, and complex caregiving situations may not be addressed adequately in a standard template. If the trust doesn't account for these nuances, it can create problems among beneficiaries.

2. Failure to Comply with State-Specific Laws

Estate planning laws, including those governing living trusts, vary from state to state. Each state has its own set of rules and requirements for creating and enforcing trusts. A **DIY template** might not be updated or tailored to comply with the specific laws in your state, making it potentially **invalid or unenforceable**.

For example:

- **Witnessing and Notarization**: Some states require trusts to be witnessed by specific individuals or notarized to be legally valid. A DIY template may not account for these requirements.
- **Tax Laws**: States have different estate tax rules, and a generic template may not account for those variations, potentially leading to tax issues down the road.
- **Trust Language**: Certain language in the trust document might not meet your state's legal requirements, rendering the document open to legal challenges.

3. Ambiguities and Lack of Clarity

A living trust is a legal document, and its language must be **precise** and **unambiguous** to ensure that your wishes are carried out exactly as intended. A template often contains vague or generalized language that leaves too much room for interpretation, which can lead to disputes among beneficiaries or even cause your trust to be contested in court.

For example, a clause like "I leave my estate to my children" may not be sufficient, as it doesn't specify how the estate should be divided, when the assets should be distributed, or what to do in the event that one of the children predeceases the grantor. Vague or unclear instructions create ambiguity and make it easier for family members to argue about the trust's intent.

4. Missing or Incomplete Provisions

A comprehensive living trust addresses several critical areas to ensure it works effectively. Some of these provisions include:

- **Successor trustee designation**
- **Incidental instructions for minor children or guardianship**
- **Dispute resolution clauses**
- **Special needs considerations for certain beneficiaries**

DIY templates often **lack critical clauses** or include **incomplete provisions.** This may result in administrative issues or disputes after your death, as your successor trustee may not have clear guidance on how to proceed. Additionally, you may not have included provisions for unforeseen circumstances, such as a child with special needs or a business that requires specific management.

For example, if you have a minor child and want to name a **guardian**, the template may not have the proper language for designating guardianship or providing for the child's care. Similarly, if you have a disabled beneficiary, a template may not adequately cover how to preserve their eligibility for government benefits while providing for their needs.

Common Template Pitfalls and How to Avoid Them

While DIY living trust templates can be an easy and inexpensive way to start planning, they often come with **significant pitfalls**. In this section, we will look at the most common issues that arise with template trusts and provide solutions to avoid these errors.

1. Using Outdated or Incomplete Templates

Estate planning templates can become outdated quickly. Changes in tax laws, estate laws, or trust regulations can render a template trust invalid or incomplete. If you download a template online or use an older form, you could be unknowingly using a document that doesn't reflect the most current legal standards.

How to Avoid This Pitfall:

- **Always use updated templates**: Make sure you're using a current version of the template, ideally from a trusted provider or legal professional.
- **Consult with an attorney**: It's advisable to have an estate planning attorney review your trust to ensure it complies with the most recent laws and regulations in your state.

2. Failing to Update Beneficiary Designations

A DIY trust template may not account for your **beneficiary designations** on life insurance policies, retirement accounts, or other financial assets. These designations often override the instructions in your will or trust, which means they need to be aligned with your trust.

How to Avoid This Pitfall:

- Regularly **review your beneficiary designations** on all financial accounts and insurance policies, ensuring they reflect your current wishes.

- If necessary, update the designations to match your trust, ensuring consistency across all your documents.

3. Not Addressing Special Circumstances

If your family dynamics are unique—whether you have blended families, a special needs child, or a beneficiary who may be financially irresponsible—a standard trust template may not provide for these circumstances. A generic template might not contain the necessary provisions to handle complex situations.

How to Avoid This Pitfall:

- **Customize the trust** to address specific needs. For example, if you have a child with special needs, include provisions that ensure the trust protects their eligibility for government benefits while providing for their care.
- **Include provisions for guardianship** of minor children or specific instructions for beneficiaries who may need extra financial support.

4. Overlooking Trust Funding

Even if you create the perfect trust document, it won't do you any good unless it is **properly funded**. Funding your trust means transferring ownership of your assets to the trust. DIY templates often don't provide adequate instructions on how to fund the trust or may not make it clear that the trust isn't effective until assets are transferred.

How to Avoid This Pitfall:

- Make sure you understand **how to transfer your assets** into the trust, including real estate, bank accounts, and investments.
- Consider working with an estate planning attorney or financial advisor to ensure that all assets are properly titled in the name of the trust.

5. Not Including a Successor Trustee

A **successor trustee** is critical in case the original trustee becomes incapacitated or passes away. If the trust does not include a successor trustee clause or does not properly designate one, your family members may face delays or complications in managing the trust after your death.

How to Avoid This Pitfall:

- **Always include a successor trustee** in your trust document and, if possible, name an alternate successor trustee as well. This ensures that there is no confusion or delay in the management of your estate when the time comes.

6. Misunderstanding the Trust's Role in Avoiding Probate

While a living trust is designed to avoid probate, many DIY templates leave out important provisions that ensure a smooth transfer of assets. If assets are not properly transferred into the trust or if the instructions for distribution are unclear, the assets may still be subject to probate, undermining the purpose of creating the trust in the first place.

How to Avoid This Pitfall:

- Be sure to transfer all **assets into the trust** during your lifetime, including real estate, bank accounts, and other personal property.
- Include clear instructions for the distribution of assets and ensure the trust is funded properly.

How to Ensure Your Trust Is Clear and Enforceable

To ensure that your trust is both clear and enforceable, it is essential to approach the process with care. This means using precise language, avoiding ambiguities, and making sure the trust complies with both state and federal laws.

Here are some steps to ensure your trust is clear and enforceable:

1. Use Clear and Precise Language

Legal documents must use **specific, unambiguous language** to ensure they are enforceable. Vague language in your trust document can lead to disputes over interpretation and ultimately cause delays in the administration of your estate.

- Avoid general terms like "my children" or "my family." Instead, specify each individual by name and clarify exactly what they will receive and when.
- Ensure that the **language** used for asset distribution, health care decisions, or trustee responsibilities is clear and precise.

2. Consult with an Estate Planning Attorney

While DIY templates can seem appealing, working with an estate planning attorney ensures that your trust is legally sound, state-specific, and tailored to your unique circumstances. An attorney can help identify potential issues, create customized provisions, and ensure that your trust complies with all necessary legal requirements.

3. Regularly Update Your Trust

As your life circumstances change—whether through marriage, divorce, the birth of children, or the acquisition of new assets—it's important to **update your trust** accordingly. Regular reviews ensure that your wishes remain accurately reflected and prevent disputes based on outdated or incomplete documents.

Simple Fixes to Common DIY Trust Mistakes

The biggest danger of using a DIY living trust template is that it may not be fully customized to your specific situation, and it may not address all the necessary provisions. Below are some of the most common mistakes people make when using DIY templates and how to fix them:

1. Failing to Fund the Trust Properly

One of the most common mistakes people make with a living trust is failing to fund it properly. A living trust is only effective if you transfer ownership of your assets into it. If you don't fund your trust by transferring your assets into it, those assets will still need to go through probate.

How to Fix This:

- **Transfer Assets into the Trust**: After creating your trust, make sure to **retitle all assets** in the name of the trust. This includes real estate, bank accounts, investments, personal property, and life insurance policies. You will need to contact financial institutions, the county recorder for real estate, and insurance companies to make these changes.
- **Review New Assets**: If you acquire new assets after creating the trust, don't forget to transfer them into the trust as well. This includes things like vehicles, business interests, or newly opened bank accounts.

The best way to ensure your trust is funded properly is to regularly review and update your assets. Failing to transfer assets could mean that some of your estate will go through probate, defeating the purpose of the living trust.

2. Ambiguous or Vague Language in Distribution Provisions

Another common mistake is using **vague or unclear language** when specifying how assets will be distributed. A living trust should leave no room for interpretation. Ambiguity or generalized terms can lead to confusion, legal challenges, and family disputes over how assets should be divided.

How to Fix This:

- **Be Specific About Beneficiaries and Assets**: Instead of saying, "I leave my estate to my children," specify exactly what each child will receive. For example, "I leave my house at [address] to [child's name], my car to [another child's name], and the remainder of my estate equally divided between my children."
- **Consider Special Gifts**: If there are specific items of sentimental or financial value, such as jewelry, artwork, or family heirlooms, make sure to list these items and specify which beneficiary will receive them. A separate **memorandum of personal property** can be attached to the trust to cover these items.

The key is to be clear, thorough, and precise in your instructions to avoid misunderstandings or disputes later on.

3. Not Addressing Special Family Dynamics

If your family dynamics are complex—such as blended families, estranged relationships, or children with special needs—a simple DIY trust template may not address these unique circumstances. This lack of consideration can lead to unintended consequences and hurt feelings.

How to Fix This:

- **Provide for Blended Families**: If you have stepchildren or children from previous marriages, you should specifically address how assets will be distributed among all children. For example, you may choose to provide a larger share to a child who has been a caregiver or a smaller share to a child who has already received gifts or support.
- **Include Provisions for Special Needs Children**: If you have a child with special needs, consider creating a **special needs trust** within your living trust. This ensures that the child's inheritance won't interfere with their eligibility for government assistance, such as

Medicaid or Supplemental Security Income (SSI).

- **Address Caregivers or Non-Family Members**: If you plan to leave assets to a non-family member or a caregiver who has helped you, include specific provisions and acknowledge their contributions. If the caregiver is a family member, clarify their role to avoid any ambiguity.

By including these special provisions in your trust, you ensure that your wishes are carried out and that all beneficiaries are treated fairly according to their unique circumstances.

4. Not Appointing a Successor Trustee

Many DIY trust templates fail to properly address the **successor trustee**. The trustee is the person responsible for managing the trust after your death or incapacity. If the trustee becomes unable or unwilling to serve, your estate could face significant delays or complications.

How to Fix This:

- **Appoint a Successor Trustee**: Always name at least one successor trustee to act in the event that the original trustee is unable or unwilling to fulfill their duties. Ideally, you should name a **primary successor trustee** and a **secondary successor trustee** in case the first choice cannot serve.
- **Consider a Neutral Trustee**: If there are concerns about family conflicts, consider naming a neutral third party, such as a financial institution, attorney, or trust company, as the trustee. This can help ensure that the trust is administered impartially.

This provision is essential to avoid court involvement and ensure the efficient management of your estate.

5. Overlooking Healthcare and Incapacity Provisions

While a living trust is primarily used to manage assets after death, it can also address issues of **incapacity**. Many DIY trusts do not include provisions for

healthcare decisions, medical care, or guardianship of minor children in the event that the grantor becomes incapacitated.

How to Fix This:

- **Add Healthcare Provisions**: Incorporate a **healthcare directive** or **living will** into your estate plan, specifying what medical treatments you would want in case you become incapacitated. This can include your preferences regarding life support, organ donation, or palliative care.
- **Incapacity Planning**: In addition to a healthcare directive, ensure your trust addresses **incapacity planning** by naming someone who will make decisions on your behalf if you are unable to do so. This could be a **power of attorney** for healthcare, which appoints a trusted individual to make medical decisions if you cannot communicate your wishes.
- **Guardianship for Minor Children**: If you have minor children, the trust should name a **guardian** to care for them if something happens to you. If you fail to address this, your children may end up in foster care or with a court-appointed guardian instead of someone you trust.

Incorporating these provisions into your estate plan helps ensure that your family's needs are met in times of crisis and that your medical and personal wishes are honored.

6. Failing to Update Your Trust Regularly

Life changes constantly. New assets are acquired, beneficiaries are added, and family dynamics evolve. One of the biggest mistakes with DIY trusts is failing to update the document regularly. If your trust no longer reflects your current life circumstances, it may not be legally valid or enforceable.

How to Fix This:

- **Review and Update Regularly**: Review your trust at least every three to five years to ensure it reflects your current wishes. Update it immediately after major life changes, such as marriage, divorce, the birth of a child, or the acquisition of new assets.

- **Document Changes Clearly**: If you need to make changes, ensure that they are documented correctly. This could involve creating an **amendment** or **restatement** of the trust to reflect the updated terms. Any amendments should be signed, notarized, and attached to the original trust document.

By regularly reviewing and updating your trust, you ensure that it remains valid and reflects your current wishes.

Why You Should Seek Legal Help for Complex Situations

While DIY living trusts can work for simple estates, **complex situations** require the expertise of an experienced estate planning attorney. If your situation involves significant assets, special family circumstances, or complicated tax planning, it is highly recommended to seek professional legal help to avoid mistakes and ensure that your trust is legally sound.

1. Customization for Complex Estates

If you have a **large estate**, a **business**, or **multiple real estate holdings**, a DIY template may not address the complexities of managing these assets. For example, if you own a family business, you may need specific provisions to ensure the business continues after your death, or you may want to create a **business succession plan** to determine who will take over.

A professional estate planner can help you structure your trust to account for these complexities and ensure the right people are in place to manage your assets.

2. Tax Planning Expertise

An estate planning attorney can provide critical insight into minimizing **estate taxes**, **capital gains taxes**, and **income taxes**. There are various strategies available, such as **irrevocable trusts**, **charitable giving strategies**, and **generation-skipping trusts**, that can help reduce the tax burden on your estate and beneficiaries. A DIY trust template likely won't cover these strategies, leaving you and your beneficiaries exposed to unnecessary tax liabilities.

3. Legal Compliance with State Laws

Estate planning laws vary significantly from state to state. A template created in one jurisdiction may not comply with the legal requirements in your state, leaving your trust invalid or open to legal challenges. An attorney will ensure that your trust is tailored to your state's specific requirements, minimizing the risk of your estate being subject to probate or tax complications.

4. Handling Family Conflicts

Estate planning is often as much about family dynamics as it is about finances. An experienced attorney can help you navigate sensitive issues, such as appointing a guardian for minor children, managing caregiving responsibilities, or handling **blended families**. By providing legal advice on how to address these issues in your trust, an attorney can help prevent conflicts and ensure your wishes are clearly understood and legally enforceable.

Chapter 10: Complete Your Trust in One Weekend

How to Get Started and Finish Quickly

The first step to completing your living trust is getting started. The idea of estate planning can feel like an intimidating mountain to climb, but once you break it down into manageable steps, the process becomes much more approachable. Here's how to quickly get started and set yourself up for success.

1. Set a Clear, Defined Goal

Before diving into the details of your living trust, set a clear goal for what you want to accomplish. It's important to define exactly what you want from your estate planning session. Are you looking to simply create a living trust, or do you also want to include other components like a will, healthcare directive, and power of attorney? These are all important components of a comprehensive estate plan, but if you are focused on completing your living trust in a weekend, keep the goal simple.

How to Do This:

- **Define your end goal**: For example, "Create a living trust and fund it with my primary assets."
- **Set realistic expectations**: Completing a comprehensive estate plan (will, power of attorney, etc.) in a weekend may be difficult, so focus on your most urgent need—creating the trust. You can always return to other elements later.
- **Break the process down**: Split the tasks into smaller chunks, and focus on completing them one by one. By the end of the weekend, your trust should be ready to go.

2. Gather the Necessary Documents

To complete your living trust, you'll need a few basic documents and pieces of information. Gathering these ahead of time will help streamline the process and save you time.

Documents You'll Need:

- **Personal Identification**: Have a valid ID (driver's license or passport) to verify your identity when signing the trust.
- **List of Assets**: Compile a list of your key assets (real estate, bank accounts, retirement accounts, life insurance policies, and business interests). You'll need to know how these assets should be distributed and to whom.
- **Beneficiaries**: Identify your beneficiaries (children, spouse, other loved ones, or charities) and decide what each will inherit.
- **Trustee and Successor Trustee Information**: Select someone you trust to manage the trust, and choose a successor trustee in case the primary trustee can't fulfill the role.
- **Legal Advice (if necessary)**: If there are any complexities, like business interests or special needs dependents, you might want to consult with an estate planning attorney. Otherwise, you can proceed with a DIY approach.

Having all of these documents prepared before you start will save you time during the actual process of creating the trust.

The Quickest Path from "I Should" to "It's Done"

Now that you're clear on your goals and have the necessary documents, it's time to take action. The key to completing your living trust in a weekend is to stay focused, avoid distractions, and stick to the schedule. Here's how to move from the "I should" stage to the "It's done" stage quickly and efficiently.

1. Allocate a Specific Time Block

Set aside a specific block of time to complete your trust. Treat it like any other important appointment, and don't let anything get in the way. For many people, a weekend is the perfect time to tackle this task, as it allows you to focus without work or other commitments.

How to Do This:

- **Schedule uninterrupted time**: Set aside 4-6 hours on both Saturday and Sunday to work on your trust. Turn off distractions like your phone or email so you can focus entirely on the task at hand.
- **Work in stages**: Break down the work into manageable parts, such as drafting the trust, selecting beneficiaries, and transferring assets. Doing a little at a time can prevent feeling overwhelmed.

By creating a designated time slot for your trust planning, you will ensure that you stay on track and make progress quickly.

2. Start with the Basics: Choose Your Trustee and Beneficiaries

The first and easiest step in the living trust creation process is selecting your **trustee** and **beneficiaries**. This is a straightforward decision, as long as you've given some thought to who will be in charge of your estate and who should benefit from it.

- **Choose a Trustee**: Your trustee will be responsible for managing the trust, so choose someone trustworthy, reliable, and capable of handling financial and legal matters. Most people choose a close family member, a friend, or a professional trustee (e.g., a bank or trust company).

- **Choose Beneficiaries**: Beneficiaries are the individuals or organizations that will inherit your estate. Be specific about what each beneficiary will receive, especially if certain assets are particularly valuable or sentimental.

3. Draft the Trust Document

The next step is drafting the actual **living trust document**. This is where you'll specify how your assets will be managed and distributed upon your death. A living trust template can help with this process, but ensure it is customized to your specific wishes.

How to Do This:

- **Use a Trust Template**: If you're doing this on your own, use a **reputable online living trust template** that is specific to your state's laws. Templates guide you through the process of creating the trust and asking the right questions to ensure all the necessary information is included.
- **Include Key Provisions**: The trust document should include details about:
  - Who will manage the trust (trustee).
  - Who will receive your assets (beneficiaries).
  - How the assets will be divided (specific bequests and percentages).
  - What happens if the trustee becomes incapacitated or unable to serve.
  - Instructions for asset management and distribution.

4. Ensure the Trust Is Legally Valid

For your living trust to be valid, it must comply with **state-specific laws**. This typically means:

- **Sign the document**: The trust must be signed by you, the grantor, in the presence of a notary.
- **Witnesses (if required)**: Depending on your state, you may need witnesses to sign the document. Make sure to follow your state's requirements to avoid issues later.
- **Record a Deed (if applicable)**: For real estate, you may need to **record a deed** to transfer the property into the trust.

5. Fund the Trust

Once the trust document is created, you need to **fund the trust** by transferring ownership of your assets into it. This is often the most time-consuming part of the process, but it's essential to ensure your trust serves its purpose of avoiding probate and efficiently managing your estate.

How to Do This:

- **Real Estate**: Contact the county recorder's office to file a **new deed** transferring real estate into the trust.
- **Bank Accounts and Investments**: Update your bank and investment accounts to reflect the trust as the account owner. This typically involves presenting a copy of your trust document to the bank or financial institution.
- **Personal Property**: For personal assets (jewelry, vehicles, etc.), you may need to create a **personal property memorandum** to specify which items go to which beneficiaries.

Time-Boxing Your Estate Planning

Time-boxing is a technique used to allocate a specific amount of time to a task and stick to that timeframe. By applying this technique to your estate planning, you can create your living trust without feeling overwhelmed or distracted. Here's how time-boxing can work for you:

1. Set Time Limits for Each Step

Instead of spending all weekend working on your trust, set specific time limits for each task. For example, you might spend the first hour gathering documents, the next two hours drafting the trust, and the final hour reviewing the trust and funding it.

How to Do This:

- **Break the work into manageable chunks**: Allocate specific times for different tasks. For example:
    - Saturday Morning: Choose your trustee, beneficiaries, and list of assets (2 hours).
    - Saturday Afternoon: Draft the living trust (3 hours).
    - Sunday Morning: Review the trust for accuracy and clarity (2 hours).
    - Sunday Afternoon: Fund the trust by transferring assets (2-3 hours).

By setting clear limits, you will avoid spending too much time on any one task and ensure that your weekend is productive.

2. Avoid Perfectionism

Estate planning is important, but it doesn't need to be perfect the first time. Remember, your goal is to create a **solid foundation** for your estate plan, not to craft an impeccable, detailed document right away. You can always revisit and update your trust later, but getting it done in a weekend sets you up to move forward with confidence.

How to Do This:

- **Focus on progress, not perfection**: Don't get bogged down by minor details or try to make everything perfect. The goal is to finish the trust by the end of the weekend.
- **Make updates later**: If you realize something needs to be adjusted or updated after completing the trust, you can always revise it at a later date.

3. Stay Focused and Minimize Distractions

Set aside time where you can work without distractions. This is a critical part of time-boxing: focusing entirely on the task at hand without interruptions. Turn off your phone, email, or social media notifications to make the most of the time you've set aside.

How to Do This:

- **Create a distraction-free environment**: Choose a quiet space, free from interruptions, where you can work on your estate planning documents.
- **Set short breaks**: Allow yourself brief breaks during your time-boxed sessions to refresh and refocus, but make sure these breaks don't turn into distractions that waste your valuable planning time.

What to Do Before You Start: Preparation is Key

Before diving into the creation of your trust, proper **preparation** is crucial. Gathering the necessary documents and identifying your goals will save time and prevent any delays during the weekend process. Here's what you need to do before you start working on your living trust:

1. List Your Assets

Start by making a comprehensive list of your assets, as the trust will need to account for each one. This includes everything you own, from real estate and investments to personal property and digital assets. Having this information at your fingertips will help you determine how to allocate your assets among beneficiaries and fund the trust effectively.

Assets to include:

- **Real estate**: Homes, rental properties, land, etc.
- **Bank accounts**: Savings, checking, and money market accounts.
- **Retirement accounts**: IRAs, 401(k)s, pensions, and other retirement funds.
- **Personal property**: Jewelry, artwork, collectibles, vehicles, etc.
- **Investment accounts**: Stocks, bonds, mutual funds, etc.
- **Life insurance policies**: Policies and their respective beneficiaries.
- **Business interests**: Ownership in businesses, stocks in a corporation, partnerships, etc.
- **Digital assets**: Social media accounts, cryptocurrencies, intellectual property, etc.

By having this list prepared, you will avoid wasting time gathering information during the process, and you'll be able to allocate your assets properly within the trust.

2. Choose Your Trustee and Successor Trustee

The next critical step in the planning process is selecting your **trustee**—the person or institution responsible for managing your trust after you pass away or become incapacitated. It's equally important to choose a **successor trustee**, who will step in if the primary trustee is unable to fulfill their duties.

Who should you choose?

- **Trustworthiness**: Your trustee must be someone who is trustworthy and reliable.
- **Organizational skills**: Since the trustee will handle your financial matters and ensure that the terms of the trust are carried out, they need to have solid organizational and financial management skills.
- **Impartiality**: If there are multiple beneficiaries, it's best to choose a trustee who can remain neutral and avoid potential conflicts.

Many people choose family members or close friends to act as trustees, but some opt for professional fiduciaries (such as a trust company or attorney), especially if the estate is large or complex.

3. Select Your Beneficiaries

Your **beneficiaries** are the individuals or organizations that will inherit your assets. This step requires careful consideration, as you will need to decide who will receive specific assets and how they will be distributed. It's essential to be clear about who receives what to avoid confusion or family disputes.

Considerations when selecting beneficiaries:

- **Family and loved ones**: Decide how to divide your estate between children, spouses, and other relatives.
- **Special gifts**: You may want to allocate specific assets (e.g., a family heirloom or business interests) to particular individuals.
- **Charitable gifts**: If you wish to leave a portion of your estate to charity, make those designations clear.
- **Contingent beneficiaries**: Designate secondary beneficiaries in case your primary beneficiaries pass away before you.

The Step-by-Step Plan to Complete Your Trust

Once you have your documents and decisions in place, you're ready to begin drafting and finalizing your trust. Below is a **step-by-step plan** for completing your trust efficiently over the course of the weekend.

Saturday Morning: Choose Your Trustee and Beneficiaries

The first step in drafting your trust is to make the fundamental decisions about who will manage your estate and who will inherit your assets.

Step 1: Choose Your Trustee(s)

- Write down the name(s) of your chosen trustee and successor trustee.
- Consider naming a professional fiduciary if your estate is large or complex.

Step 2: Choose Your Beneficiaries

- List the names of your beneficiaries and decide what each person will receive.
- Be specific about the division of your estate, especially if you are leaving items of personal or sentimental value.

Step 3: Outline Specific Requests or Bequests

- Think about any special instructions you'd like to include for specific assets. This could be a family heirloom, an art collection, or even a specific amount of money allocated to a cause or charity.

Saturday Afternoon: Draft the Trust Document

Now that you've selected the individuals who will manage and benefit from your trust, it's time to start drafting the actual document. You can use a reputable **online trust template** or work with an attorney to ensure that the trust is legally sound.

Step 1: Use a Trust Template

- If you're creating the trust on your own, use a **reliable, state-specific trust template** to ensure compliance with local laws.
- The template will guide you through questions like who will be the trustee, what assets are being transferred, how assets will be distributed, and who the beneficiaries are.

Step 2: Include Provisions for Incapacity

- Include a section that addresses incapacity planning, designating who will make financial or healthcare decisions if you are unable to do so.

Step 3: Detail Special Provisions

- If you have special circumstances (like a child with special needs or a business you want to be handled in a particular way), be sure to include specific instructions to address these concerns.

Sunday Morning: Sign, Notarize, and Witness the Trust

Once the trust document is complete, it needs to be legally executed to be valid. While the specific requirements can vary from state to state, most living trusts need to be signed by the **grantor** (you) in the presence of witnesses and/or a notary.

Step 1: Sign the Trust Document

- Sign the trust document in front of a **notary public** to ensure it is legally valid.
- Some states may require additional witnesses to sign the trust, so make sure you are in compliance with your state's specific requirements.

Step 2: Notarization

- A notary public will verify your identity and ensure that you are signing the document voluntarily. This step is often required for legal validity.

Step 3: Make Copies

- Once the trust is signed and notarized, make several copies. Give copies to your trustee, attorney (if applicable), and any other individuals who should have access to the trust.

Sunday Afternoon: Fund Your Trust and Finalize the Process

Now that your living trust document is signed and notarized, the final step is to ensure that it is **properly funded**. Funding your trust means transferring the ownership of your assets to the trust so they can be managed and distributed according to the terms of the trust.

Step 1: Transfer Ownership of Assets

- For **real estate**, you'll need to file a **new deed** with the county recorder to transfer the property into the name of the trust.
- For **bank accounts**, contact your bank to retitle the accounts in the name of the trust.
- For **investment accounts**, transfer ownership of stocks, bonds, and other investments to the trust by working with your financial institution.
- For **personal property**, create a **personal property memorandum** that lists valuable items and specifies who will receive them.

Step 2: Update Beneficiary Designations

- If you have life insurance policies, retirement accounts, or other assets with designated beneficiaries, update these designations to reflect your trust as the primary or contingent beneficiary.

Step 3: Store Your Trust Safely

- Once your trust is funded, keep the original document in a safe place, such as a fireproof safe or safe deposit box. Ensure that your trustee and other relevant parties know where to find the document in case it is needed.

Step 4: Communicate with Your Family

- Let your family and beneficiaries know that your living trust is complete. Provide them with basic information about how it works, who is named as the trustee, and what they can expect.

Time-Boxing Your Estate Planning

Time-boxing is an effective technique that helps you stay on track and complete your trust without getting overwhelmed. By setting clear time limits for each task, you can focus on completing one step at a time, keeping you focused and productive.

Time-Boxing Steps for Completing Your Trust:

- **Saturday Morning**: Spend 2-3 hours selecting your trustee and beneficiaries, reviewing your asset list, and outlining specific bequests.
- **Saturday Afternoon**: Dedicate 3-4 hours to drafting the trust document, either with a template or working with an attorney if necessary.
- **Sunday Morning**: Allocate 1-2 hours for signing, notarizing, and making copies of the document.
- **Sunday Afternoon**: Spend 2-3 hours transferring assets into the trust and updating beneficiary designations.

What to Do After You Finish Your Trust

Once your living trust is complete, it's important to ensure that it remains effective and up-to-date. Estate planning is an ongoing process, and there are several steps you should take after your trust is finished:

1. Review Your Trust Regularly

- Estate plans should be reviewed regularly, especially after major life events like marriage, divorce, the birth of children, or the acquisition of new assets.

- Update your trust whenever necessary to reflect changes in your family or financial situation.

2. Inform Your Successor Trustee

- Make sure your successor trustee knows they have been named and understands their role. Give them a copy of the trust and ensure they are familiar with your wishes.

3. Communicate Your Wishes to Family Members

- While it may be uncomfortable, it's important to have open discussions with your family members about the trust. Let them know your intentions and reassure them that your plan is in place.

4. Keep Your Trust Funded

- Regularly check that new assets are transferred into the trust. If you acquire new property or assets, make sure they are added to the trust promptly.

Chapter 11: Funding and Maintaining Your Trust

What It Means to Fund Your Trust and Why It's Essential

One of the most important steps in the estate planning process is funding your living trust. This term refers to the process of transferring ownership of your assets to the trust you've created. Without properly funding your trust, it will not serve its purpose of bypassing probate, keeping your assets out of the public eye, and ensuring a smooth and efficient transfer of assets to your beneficiaries.

Why Funding Your Trust Is Crucial

When you create a living trust, it's essentially a **legal entity** that can own property, manage assets, and distribute wealth. The trust itself holds no assets until you transfer ownership of your assets to it. Funding your trust ensures that everything you want to pass on to your heirs is covered by the trust's provisions.

Without proper funding, your trust becomes little more than a piece of paper with no practical effect. If assets are not transferred into the trust, they will be considered part of your estate, which may be subject to **probate**—a time-consuming and expensive legal process. Probate involves a court proceeding in which the decedent's assets are distributed according to the will (or, in the absence of a will, state law), and it can take months or even years to complete. Furthermore, probate is a public process, which means the details of your estate will become accessible to anyone.

By funding your trust, you ensure that your assets are protected from probate and are distributed according to your instructions. It also gives your trustee the legal authority to manage and distribute assets without delay, which provides peace of mind to both you and your beneficiaries.

How to Fund Your Trust

Funding your trust involves transferring the ownership of assets from your name into the name of the trust. This process varies depending on the type of asset involved, but generally, it follows these steps:

1. **Real Estate**: If you own real estate, such as a home, rental properties, or land, you must transfer the title of the property into the name of the trust. This is done by preparing and recording a **deed** with your county recorder's office. The deed should state that the property is being transferred from your personal name to the name of the trust.

For example, the deed should read:
"I, [Grantor's Name], transfer ownership of the property located at [Property Address] to the [Trust Name], dated [Date]."

1. **Bank Accounts**: For bank accounts, the process usually involves visiting your bank or financial institution and asking them to retitle the account in the name of the trust. Some banks may require you to present a copy of the trust document to verify that the trust exists and is properly funded.
2. **Investment Accounts**: Investment accounts, such as stocks, bonds, mutual funds, and retirement accounts, need to be transferred into the trust. For stocks and bonds, this typically means contacting your brokerage firm and instructing them to transfer ownership to the trust. Be sure to include the trust's name and date to avoid confusion.
3. **Personal Property**: Personal property, such as jewelry, artwork, and vehicles, can be transferred into the trust using a **personal property memorandum**. This is an informal document that lists specific items and their intended recipients. While you don't necessarily need to retitle personal property in the name of the trust, creating a detailed inventory ensures that your wishes are clear and legally enforceable.
4. **Life Insurance Policies**: Life insurance policies should be transferred to the trust as well, or you should name the trust as the **beneficiary** of

the policy. This ensures that the life insurance proceeds are distributed directly to the trust, allowing for a smoother transition of assets to your beneficiaries.

5. **Business Interests**: If you own a business, you must transfer the business interests or shares into the trust. This could involve updating your business's operating agreement or articles of incorporation to reflect the trust as the new owner.

The Correct Way to Retitle Your Assets

Retitling assets is one of the most crucial parts of funding your trust. This means changing the legal ownership of your assets from your name to the name of the trust. Without this step, the assets are not part of the trust, and they could be subject to probate.

Real Estate

Transferring real estate into your trust is done by preparing a **new deed**. The deed should be signed by you and filed with the local county recorder's office. It's important to make sure the deed includes the legal description of the property, which is typically available from your property tax documents or your mortgage lender.

- **Types of Deeds**: You'll generally use a **quitclaim deed** or a **warranty deed** to transfer the property into the trust. The difference between these two types of deeds lies in the level of guarantee provided. A quitclaim deed transfers the property without any warranties, while a warranty deed guarantees that you have clear title to the property.
- **Recording the Deed**: Once signed, the deed must be recorded with the county or city where the property is located. This makes the transfer of ownership official and publicly recognized.

Bank and Financial Accounts

Retitling bank and financial accounts involves notifying your bank or financial institution that you want to transfer the account into the trust. Banks usually require you to provide a copy of the trust agreement and other documentation, such as identification, before they will retitle the account. In many cases, they will simply add the name of the trust as a co-owner on the account.

- **Beneficiary Designations**: For assets like retirement accounts or life insurance, you may not need to retitle the accounts themselves. Instead, you can name the trust as the **primary or contingent beneficiary** of the asset. This ensures that, upon your death, the assets in those accounts will pass directly to the trust.

Personal Property

For personal property like jewelry, artwork, or collectibles, creating a **personal property memorandum** is an effective way to ensure that these items are included in the trust. The memorandum can list specific items, their value, and the person to whom each item should go. While the memorandum is not legally required to be notarized, it is important that it is signed by you, the grantor, to ensure its enforceability.

What to Leave Out of Your Trust

While a living trust is an excellent tool for managing many types of assets, not all assets should be included in the trust. In some cases, it may be better to keep assets out of the trust, either because of legal or practical reasons. Here are some types of assets that you may want to exclude from your trust:

1. Retirement Accounts (IRAs, 401(k)s, etc.)

Retirement accounts, such as **IRAs**, **401(k)s**, and pensions, should not be transferred into your living trust. Instead, these accounts should have a **beneficiary designation** that names the trust as the beneficiary.

The reason for this is that retirement accounts have **tax-deferred status**, and transferring them into a trust could result in **tax penalties** or loss of tax benefits. Additionally, retirement accounts are governed by specific rules that are better managed by beneficiary designations rather than through the trust.

2. Life Insurance Policies

Similar to retirement accounts, **life insurance policies** should not be retitled in the name of your trust. Instead, you should designate the trust as the **beneficiary** of the policy. This ensures that the proceeds from your life insurance policy are paid directly to the trust, where they can be managed and distributed according to your wishes.

3. Jointly Owned Property

If you own property **jointly** with another person, such as a spouse, it's often unnecessary to transfer this property into your trust. For instance, if you and your spouse own a home as **joint tenants with right of survivorship**, the property will automatically pass to the surviving spouse upon the death of the other. Transferring this type of property into a trust may not provide any added benefit and could complicate the situation.

4. Vehicles and Personal Belongings

While vehicles can technically be transferred into a trust, it's often unnecessary, especially if they are of relatively low value. You can leave instructions for how vehicles should be handled in your **personal property memorandum** or your will. This ensures that there is no confusion about who should inherit the vehicle when the time comes.

5. Bank Accounts with Payable-on-Death (POD) Designations

If you have bank accounts with **payable-on-death (POD)** designations, these accounts will automatically transfer to the named beneficiary when you pass away. Since they do not go through probate, they do not need to be placed in your living trust. However, you should ensure that the POD designation aligns with the overall plan for your estate.

Maintaining Your Trust

Once your trust is funded, it's important to maintain it regularly to ensure it remains effective. This includes updating it as your life changes and ensuring that new assets are added. Here are the key steps for maintaining your living trust:

1. Review Your Trust Regularly

Estate plans should be reviewed regularly to ensure that they still reflect your wishes. Life changes such as marriage, divorce, the birth of children, or the acquisition of new assets may require updates to your trust. Set aside time every few years to review your trust and make any necessary adjustments.

2. Add New Assets to Your Trust

Whenever you acquire new assets, such as property, investments, or a new business, make sure to **transfer them into the trust**. Keeping the trust funded is an ongoing responsibility that requires regular updates.

3. Update Beneficiaries

If your family dynamic changes—such as the addition of new children or grandchildren, or changes in relationships—make sure to update your beneficiary designations to reflect your new wishes.

How to Review and Update Your Trust Regularly

As part of effective estate planning, it's essential to periodically review and update your living trust to ensure that it accurately reflects your current circumstances and intentions. Here's how you can maintain an up-to-date and functioning trust.

1. Schedule Regular Reviews

Just as you would review your financial situation or retirement plan, your living trust requires regular attention. Life changes, new assets, and family dynamics can all impact your estate plan, so it's vital to schedule regular **reviews** to ensure that your trust is still in line with your goals. A good rule of thumb is to review your trust at least every **three to five years.**

Key Life Events to Trigger a Review:

- **Marriage or Divorce**: If you marry or divorce, your trust may need to be updated to reflect your new spouse or to remove a former spouse from the plan.
- **Birth or Adoption of Children**: If you have new children or grandchildren, your trust should include provisions for them, such as who will be their guardian or how assets will be distributed.
- **Significant Changes in Assets**: If your financial situation changes significantly—whether through acquiring new assets, selling a major property, or experiencing substantial loss or debt—your trust may need to be revised to reflect these changes.
- **Death of a Beneficiary or Trustee**: If someone named in your trust, such as a beneficiary or trustee, passes away, you'll need to appoint a new person to carry out your wishes.
- **Health Changes**: If you or someone named in your trust becomes incapacitated or experiences a health change, your estate plan may need adjustments to account for those needs.

2. Update Your Trust When Your Family Dynamics Change

Family dynamics are often one of the most important factors in determining how your estate will be distributed. As family relationships evolve, so should your trust. If you've experienced major changes in your family life, such as a new marriage, the birth of children, or estrangement from family members, it's important to update your trust to ensure that your wishes are clearly stated.

Family Changes to Address in Your Trust:

- **Blended Families**: If you have remarried and have stepchildren, or if you have children from previous marriages, you may need to update your trust to reflect these changes. You may need to specify how assets will be divided among biological children, stepchildren, or children from previous marriages.
- **Estrangement or Changing Relationships**: If you've become estranged from a family member or have a change in relationship with someone named in your trust, you may need to revise the terms of your trust. This includes removing or replacing beneficiaries, trustees, or even guardians for minor children.
- **Designating a Guardian**: If you've had a child or wish to change the guardian for your minor children, make sure your trust clearly designates the new guardian.

3. Revisit Your Asset Distribution

As time passes, the assets in your estate may change. For example, you may acquire new assets, such as a second home, an investment property, or valuable items like artwork. Conversely, you may sell or give away assets that were originally included in your trust. These changes require an update to your trust to ensure that your assets are distributed according to your wishes.

What to Do:

- **Add New Assets**: If you acquire new assets, like real estate or investments, make sure to transfer them into your trust. This process is known as **funding your trust** and is necessary for the trust to be effective.

- **Remove Assets**: If you sell or dispose of assets, make sure to remove them from the trust or update your asset list accordingly.
- **Reassign Property**: If you have specific bequests (like jewelry or family heirlooms) designated to certain beneficiaries, you may need to update your trust if your intentions change.

4. Review Your Beneficiary Designations

While the trust dictates the overall distribution of your estate, many assets—like retirement accounts, life insurance policies, and investment accounts—are not automatically included in the trust. These assets pass based on the **beneficiary designations** attached to them.

To ensure consistency with your living trust, **review and update** beneficiary designations regularly. This includes confirming that the trust is listed as a beneficiary where appropriate and adjusting your designations if family dynamics change.

- **Retirement Accounts and Life Insurance**: Ensure that the trust is listed as the beneficiary for life insurance policies, 401(k) accounts, IRAs, and other retirement accounts. If a beneficiary is no longer in your life or you wish to change the distribution, update the beneficiary forms to reflect your new wishes.

What Happens If You Don't Fund Your Trust Correctly

Funding your trust is one of the most important steps in estate planning, but it's also one of the most commonly overlooked aspects. If you don't fund your trust correctly, it will not function as intended, and the assets that you intended to keep out of probate may end up going through the court process. Here are the consequences of failing to fund your trust properly:

1. Your Assets May Be Subject to Probate

If you don't transfer ownership of assets into your trust, those assets will not be included in the trust and will have to go through the probate process when you pass away. Probate is a **time-consuming, public**, and potentially expensive legal process in which the court oversees the distribution of your estate. The more assets you leave out of the trust, the more likely your loved ones will face the delay and expense of probate.

Why This Happens:

- **Unfunded Trusts**: If you neglect to transfer assets into your trust, those assets will remain in your name, and they will be subject to probate when you die. For example, if you have a bank account that isn't retitled in the name of the trust, it will need to go through probate.
- **The Importance of Proper Titling**: Even if you create a trust, simply signing the document isn't enough. You must also title your assets in the name of the trust (or designate the trust as the beneficiary) to ensure they avoid probate.

2. Potential Delays and Legal Disputes

When your assets are not funded into the trust, the process of managing and distributing your estate can be delayed. This can cause unnecessary emotional stress and financial hardship for your family, especially if they rely on the estate for support or if assets are tied up in probate for a long period.

Delays and Disputes:

- **Probate Court Delays**: Probate can take months, even years, depending on the complexity of your estate and the court system in your area. This process delays the distribution of assets, leading to frustration and uncertainty for your heirs.
- **Family Disputes**: Without clear instructions in the trust document and the proper funding, family members may dispute asset distribution, leading to costly litigation and potential rifts within the family.

3. Increased Costs

Probate comes with significant costs, including court fees, attorney fees, and administrative costs. If you fail to fund your trust properly, your estate will incur these costs, which could otherwise be avoided. Additionally, there may be fees associated with transferring assets into the trust after your death, which can further reduce the value of your estate.

Costs to Consider:

- **Probate Fees**: The probate process is expensive. In many states, probate court charges fees based on the size of your estate, and you'll also need to pay for legal and administrative fees.
- **Asset Transfer Costs**: If assets need to be transferred into the trust after your death, this could require additional paperwork and legal fees.

4. Uncertainty About Who Gets What

Without a properly funded trust, there can be **confusion** about who is entitled to your assets. This uncertainty may lead to disputes among family members and could result in assets being distributed in a way that you did not intend. For example, if you don't include a specific piece of property in your trust, it might end up being divided in a way that creates conflict among your heirs.

How to Avoid This:

- Ensure that **all** of your assets are properly funded into the trust before you pass away. Double-check that you've transferred ownership of real estate, bank accounts, investment portfolios, life insurance policies, and other valuable assets to the trust.
- If you are unsure of how to transfer certain assets, consult an estate planning attorney who can guide you through the process.

What to Leave Out of Your Trust

While it's essential to fund your trust with most of your assets, there are certain assets that you should **leave out** of the trust. These assets may not require funding, or they may have special rules regarding their transfer. Here are some examples of what to leave out:

1. Retirement Accounts and Life Insurance Policies

As mentioned earlier, **retirement accounts** and **life insurance policies** should not be transferred into a living trust. These assets generally have **beneficiary designations**, and the trust should be named as the beneficiary, not the owner. This ensures that the assets go directly to the trust upon your death and bypass probate.

2. Jointly Owned Property

If you own property with someone else, such as a spouse, as **joint tenants with right of survivorship**, the property will automatically pass to the surviving joint tenant upon your death. Because of this automatic transfer, you don't need to transfer this property into your trust.

3. Assets That Don't Require Probate

Some assets, such as **payable-on-death accounts** (POD accounts) or **transfer-on-death** (TOD) accounts, automatically pass to a designated beneficiary upon your death without the need for probate or a trust. These accounts do not need to be placed in your trust, as they are already structured to transfer directly to the beneficiary.

Chapter 12: Business Succession and Special Assets

Planning for Your Business: Succession and Continuity

Running a business involves much more than just managing day-to-day operations. A successful business owner must also think ahead to ensure the long-term health of the company, especially when it comes time to hand it off to the next generation or leadership team. Business succession planning is a structured process that helps business owners transition leadership and ownership in a way that protects the interests of both the business and its stakeholders.

1. What is Business Succession Planning?

Business succession planning is the process of preparing for the eventual transfer of ownership and management of a business. Succession plans are crucial because they ensure that, when the time comes, the business will continue to operate smoothly without interruption. Succession planning involves identifying potential leaders, training them, and putting the necessary structures in place to facilitate the transition of ownership and control.

Key Components of Business Succession Planning:

- **Leadership Continuity**: Identifying the right individual(s) to take over leadership and management.
- **Ownership Transition**: Determining how ownership of the business will transfer and how to value the business for the purpose of the transfer.
- **Legal and Financial Structures**: Setting up the legal frameworks that will facilitate the succession, including legal documents like wills, trusts, and buy-sell agreements.
- **Tax and Estate Considerations**: Developing a tax-efficient strategy for passing on the business, reducing estate taxes, and ensuring the financial health of the company.

Succession planning isn't just about naming a successor. It also involves making critical decisions about the company's future direction and how it will continue to thrive in the hands of new leadership.

2. Why Business Succession Planning is Essential

A well-thought-out business succession plan is essential for several reasons:

- **Ensures Continuity**: A clear plan helps ensure that the business continues to operate smoothly and meets its financial goals. Without a plan, the company could experience a sudden leadership void, which may lead to confusion, mismanagement, and financial setbacks.
- **Protects the Value of the Business**: If the transition is not planned properly, the company's value could be diminished. Effective succession planning helps maintain the value of the business and prevent disruption that could harm its reputation or customer relationships.
- **Provides Financial Security for the Owner and Family**: Business owners often tie their financial well-being to their businesses. A good succession plan ensures that they can step away from the business or retire without jeopardizing their personal financial security or the financial security of their family.
- **Prevents Family Disputes**: Business succession planning is especially important in family-owned businesses. Without a clear plan, there can be disagreements and conflicts among family members about who should take over or how the business should be divided.

3. Key Steps in Creating a Business Succession Plan

Creating a comprehensive business succession plan requires careful consideration and several key steps:

Step 1: Define Your Succession Goals

Before you can develop a plan, it's important to define your goals. Ask yourself:

- What do you want the future of your business to look like?
- Do you want to sell your business or pass it on to family members?
- Are you looking for a partial or full exit?

Clarifying these goals will guide the rest of the planning process.

Step 2: Identify and Prepare a Successor

Identify potential leaders within or outside the organization. Consider internal candidates first, as they are often familiar with the company culture and operations. However, external candidates may also be suitable depending on the direction you want for the company.

Once identified, provide them with the necessary training, mentorship, and leadership experience to prepare them for the role. If you are grooming a family member, consider their qualifications and interest in leading the company.

Step 3: Establish a Clear Timeline

Establish a timeline for the transition process. Some business owners prefer a gradual transition, while others may wish for an immediate transfer. A timeline ensures that all parties involved are prepared and that the transition is not rushed.

Step 4: Address Financial and Tax Considerations

Consult with a financial advisor or estate planning attorney to develop a strategy for the financial aspects of the business transition. This may include life insurance, buy-sell agreements, or tax-efficient strategies for minimizing capital gains and estate taxes.

Step 5: Draft Legal Documents

Work with an attorney to create the necessary legal documents, such as a **buy-sell agreement** (which outlines how the business will be sold or transferred) or a **living trust** to pass ownership to heirs or new owners. Legal documents are essential to make the succession official and enforceable.

Step 6: Communicate the Plan to Key Stakeholders

Once the plan is in place, communicate it clearly to family members, employees, and other key stakeholders. Transparent communication helps avoid misunderstandings and ensures that everyone is on the same page.

Special Considerations for Out-of-State or Overseas Assets

In addition to planning for business succession, it's equally important to address the management and transfer of **special assets** in your estate plan. Special assets can include real estate, intellectual property, and business interests that are located outside your home state or country. These assets often require specific legal and tax planning to ensure they are properly handled.

1. Out-of-State Assets

If you own property or other assets in different states, these assets may be subject to **different laws** and **taxes** than your primary residence. This is particularly relevant for **real estate**, as each state has its own set of property laws, tax rates, and inheritance rules.

Challenges of Out-of-State Assets:

- **Probate Complications**: When you have property in multiple states, probate may be required in each state, which can lead to delays, additional costs, and complications. For example, your property in your home state might be handled by a local court, while your out-of-state property could require a second probate process.
- **Tax Issues**: Different states have different inheritance and estate tax laws, which could affect how your out-of-state property is taxed. Some states have no estate taxes, while others impose significant taxes on large estates.

How to Address Out-of-State Assets:

- **Create a Separate Trust for Each State**: In some cases, it may be beneficial to create a separate **revocable living trust** for each state where you own property. This can help avoid the need for probate in multiple states.
- **Establish a Beneficiary Designation for Real Estate**: For properties

in different states, you may be able to add them to your trust's beneficiary designation to avoid probate.
- **Consult with a Local Attorney**: Since state laws vary, it's a good idea to work with an attorney in each state where you own property to ensure that everything is handled properly.

2. Overseas Assets

When it comes to **overseas assets**, the complexity increases due to differences in international laws and tax implications. You may own property abroad, or you may have business interests or investments in foreign countries. Managing these assets in your estate plan requires understanding both the legal framework of your home country and the country in which the assets are located.

Challenges of Overseas Assets:

- **Jurisdictional Issues**: Different countries have different rules regarding inheritance, property rights, and taxation. The laws in the country where the asset is located will often take precedence over the laws of your home country.
- **Currency and Tax Implications**: If you own property or financial assets overseas, their value may fluctuate with the exchange rate. Additionally, different countries may have estate, inheritance, or capital gains taxes that could apply to the transfer of assets upon your death.
- **Complicated Transfer Procedures**: Some countries may require specific legal procedures for transferring assets, such as property or business ownership. This may involve local probate or the appointment of a legal representative in that country.

How to Address Overseas Assets:

- **Consult an International Estate Planning Attorney**: Work with an attorney who specializes in **international estate planning** to ensure that your assets are handled in compliance with the laws of both your home country and the foreign country where the asset is located.

- **Create an International Will or Trust**: You may need a separate will or trust for your overseas assets, as some countries do not recognize foreign trusts or wills. Make sure that any international documents are consistent with your home country's estate plan.
- **Designate an Executor or Trustee for International Assets**: If you own significant assets abroad, consider appointing an executor or trustee with knowledge of the foreign country's legal and financial systems. This person can ensure that your international assets are transferred according to your wishes.

Protecting Digital Assets: Social Media, Cryptocurrencies, and More

With the growing role of the internet and digital technologies in our daily lives, **digital assets** have become a significant part of modern estates. These assets can range from **social media profiles** and **cryptocurrencies** to **online business interests** and **digital intellectual property**. However, most people don't realize that, just like physical assets, these digital possessions need to be carefully managed in an estate plan to avoid complications after death.

1. What Are Digital Assets?

Digital assets are any online assets that you own or have control over. They can include:

- **Social Media Accounts**: Facebook, Twitter, Instagram, LinkedIn, etc.
- **Cryptocurrencies**: Bitcoin, Ethereum, and other digital currencies.
- **Online Business Accounts**: Domains, websites, and e-commerce stores.
- **Digital Media**: Photos, videos, writings, and intellectual property stored on digital platforms.
- **Email Accounts**: Gmail, Yahoo, or any personal email account.
- **Cloud Storage**: Files stored on services like Google Drive, Dropbox, or iCloud.

These assets can hold sentimental value (such as family photos or social media posts) or financial value (such as cryptocurrencies or online business income). Without a clear plan in place, managing these assets after death can be complicated. Social media accounts can become dormant, cryptocurrencies may be lost, and digital businesses may stagnate without proper management.

2. Why You Need to Include Digital Assets in Your Estate Plan

Failing to plan for your digital assets can result in **unauthorized access** to your accounts, the loss of important data, or complications for your beneficiaries. Here are a few reasons why it's critical to include digital assets in your estate plan:

- **Access Control**: Digital assets like social media accounts and email accounts are protected by **passwords** and **security questions**. If you don't leave instructions or access information, your loved ones may be unable to access your accounts.
- **Preservation of Digital Wealth**: Cryptocurrencies like Bitcoin are stored in **digital wallets**. Without access to these wallets or a plan for transferring ownership, your cryptocurrency could be permanently lost, potentially costing your beneficiaries significant financial value.
- **Continuity of Online Businesses**: If you run an online business or have digital properties that generate income, such as websites, blogs, or e-commerce stores, your beneficiaries may not know how to manage or continue these businesses after your passing.

3. How to Protect and Manage Your Digital Assets

Including digital assets in your estate plan requires thoughtful consideration and specific planning. Here are some steps you can take to ensure your digital assets are properly protected:

Step 1: List Your Digital Assets

The first step is to create a detailed list of all your digital assets. This should include:

- Social media accounts
- Email accounts and passwords
- Cryptocurrency holdings and wallets
- Online businesses or websites you own
- Cloud storage services
- Any other digital property you want to pass on

By having this list ready, your family or executor will have a clear idea of what assets need to be managed and transferred.

Step 2: Provide Access Information

Once you've identified your digital assets, it's essential to provide access information. This could include:

- **Usernames and passwords** for social media, email accounts, and online platforms.
- **Private keys or seed phrases** for cryptocurrency wallets.
- **Login credentials** for online businesses and e-commerce platforms.
- **Instructions** for how to access your cloud storage, files, or media libraries.

The most secure way to store this information is in a **password manager**. However, you should also consider leaving a **written record** with your **executor** or a **trusted family member** who can manage your accounts if necessary. Ensure that your digital access information is stored securely but is also available to the right people after your death.

Step 3: Set Up a Digital Executor

A **digital executor** is someone specifically designated to manage your digital assets after your death. This person will be responsible for ensuring that your digital accounts are properly handled, passwords are managed, and assets are distributed according to your wishes.

When selecting a digital executor, consider someone who is tech-savvy, trustworthy, and capable of dealing with your digital affairs. You should also provide this person with the necessary access information to your digital assets, along with clear instructions for managing or transferring them.

Step 4: Address Digital Assets in Your Will or Trust

You should clearly specify how your digital assets should be handled in your will or trust. For example, you may want your social media accounts to be deleted after your passing, or you may wish to pass on your cryptocurrency holdings to your children or a charity. Make sure to:

- **Appoint a digital executor** in your will or trust.
- **Specify the distribution** of your digital assets, if applicable.

- Include any **instructions for digital asset preservation** (e.g., continuing an online business or preserving social media accounts).

Ensure that your estate plan reflects your wishes for digital assets and provides enough information to facilitate their management.

4. The Special Case of Cryptocurrencies

Cryptocurrencies are a relatively new asset class that presents unique challenges in estate planning. Unlike traditional assets, cryptocurrencies are stored in **digital wallets** that are protected by **private keys** or **seed phrases**. If these private keys are lost or inaccessible, the cryptocurrency is essentially gone.

To ensure that your cryptocurrency is passed on effectively, you should:

- **Keep a written record** of your private keys or seed phrases in a secure location (e.g., a safety deposit box or password manager).
- **Designate a cryptocurrency executor** who understands how to manage and transfer cryptocurrency after your death.
- **Specify your wishes** for how your cryptocurrency should be handled (whether to sell, transfer, or hold the assets).

How to Include Family Businesses in Your Estate Plan

In addition to digital assets, **family businesses** require special consideration in your estate plan. Passing down a family business can be a complex process, as it involves not only the transfer of ownership but also the continuation of operations, management, and potentially the preservation of family relationships. Without a clear plan, the business could face financial, operational, and interpersonal challenges.

1. Why Business Succession Planning Matters for Family Businesses

Family businesses are often built with years of hard work and are an essential source of income and livelihood for multiple generations. When the business owner dies or becomes incapacitated, it's important to have a clear plan to ensure that the business continues operating smoothly. Without a succession plan, the business may fall into disarray, leading to a loss of value, business disruption, and even family conflict.

Business succession planning helps ensure:

- **Continuity of the business**: The company continues to run smoothly without interruption.
- **Preservation of wealth**: The value of the business is maintained, and taxes and legal costs are minimized.
- **Clarity in ownership**: The next generation of owners is clearly identified, and responsibilities are defined.

2. Key Components of Business Succession Planning

A comprehensive business succession plan for a family business should include the following components:

- **Identification of Successors**: Identify who will take over the business when you are no longer able to manage it. This could include children, other family members, or trusted employees. It's essential to choose individuals who are capable of running the business and have the necessary skills and interest.

- **Training and Development**: Successors need to be adequately prepared for leadership roles. This involves providing them with the training, mentorship, and leadership experience necessary to run the business effectively. Succession planning should start early, ideally while you are still actively managing the business.
- **Ownership Transfer**: Define how ownership will transfer. Will you sell the business to the next generation, pass it on as a gift, or use a trust to manage the transfer? The method of transfer will impact taxes and the value of the business.
- **Buy-Sell Agreements**: If there are multiple family members or business partners involved, a **buy-sell agreement** can be crucial. This agreement outlines what happens if one of the business owners wants to exit, becomes incapacitated, or passes away. It can help prevent disputes over ownership and ensure that the business continues to operate smoothly.
- **Estate Tax Considerations**: Business succession planning involves addressing potential estate tax liabilities. Depending on the value of your business, your estate could be subject to significant taxes upon your death. Work with an estate planning attorney and financial advisor to develop tax strategies that minimize the estate tax burden on your heirs.

3. Integrating the Family Business into Your Trust

Your family business should be included in your **living trust** to avoid probate and ensure the smooth transfer of ownership. The trust can specify how the business should be handled upon your death, including appointing a new owner or manager. Here's how to integrate your business into your estate plan:

- **Transfer Business Ownership to the Trust**: Just like real estate or personal property, the ownership of your business should be transferred into the trust. If your business is incorporated, this may involve transferring shares of stock to the trust. If it's a partnership, ownership interests will need to be assigned to the trust.

- **Specify Succession and Management in the Trust**: Clearly outline who will manage the business and how ownership will be transferred. You can also include provisions for managing the business until the successor is ready to take control.
- **Provide for the Financial Interests of Family Members**: If you have multiple children or heirs, your trust should clearly specify how the business profits or equity will be divided, ensuring that your estate plan addresses the interests of all beneficiaries.

Chapter 13: Trusts for Your Loved Ones

How to Educate Your Beneficiaries About Your Trust

A trust is a legal document that outlines how your assets will be managed and distributed after your death. But having a solid trust in place is only part of the equation. If your beneficiaries do not understand how the trust functions or what is expected of them, it can lead to confusion, delays, and even legal disputes. The goal of educating your beneficiaries is to empower them with the knowledge they need to ensure that the trust is administered properly, according to your wishes.

1. Why Communication is Key

Clear communication is vital for a smooth estate administration process. Beneficiaries often find themselves navigating a complicated legal and financial process after the death of a loved one. The grief and stress of the situation can make understanding the trust's provisions even more difficult. When beneficiaries are informed and prepared, they are better equipped to handle the responsibilities that come with inheriting assets.

Benefits of Educating Beneficiaries:

- **Reduces Conflict**: When beneficiaries understand your intentions and the terms of the trust, there is less room for disputes and misunderstandings.
- **Ensures Compliance with Your Wishes**: By making sure your beneficiaries know exactly what you want, they are more likely to carry out your wishes effectively.
- **Prevents Unnecessary Delays**: If beneficiaries know what steps to take after your death, they can quickly move forward with the necessary administrative processes.
- **Prevents Legal Challenges**: Lack of understanding can sometimes lead beneficiaries to challenge the trust in court, which can be time-consuming and costly. Educating them reduces the likelihood of this happening.

2. Who Should Be Informed About the Trust?

One of the first questions you'll need to address is **who** should be informed about the trust. Ideally, you want to ensure that **key individuals** are aware of the trust's existence and understand their roles.

Key individuals to inform:

- **Trustees**: Your trustee is the person or entity responsible for managing the trust after your death or incapacity. They need to understand their duties and responsibilities fully. Make sure the trustee knows where the trust document is located, and that they are familiar with the terms and provisions of the trust.
- **Beneficiaries**: Beneficiaries are the individuals or entities that will inherit from the trust. These people should be informed of their status as beneficiaries and should have a clear understanding of what they are entitled to and how the assets will be distributed.
- **Family Members**: In some cases, it may be helpful to inform other family members, especially if there are specific provisions in the trust related to them (such as a guardian for minor children or special instructions for a family business). This can help avoid misunderstandings or hurt feelings in the future.
- **Advisors**: It is also important to inform your financial advisor, tax professional, or attorney, as they may need to provide assistance with managing or distributing the trust's assets.

3. How to Inform Your Beneficiaries

The next step is to **communicate the details of the trust** to your beneficiaries. It's essential to approach this conversation carefully to ensure clarity and understanding. The conversation should be done in a calm and organized manner, considering the emotional aspect of the situation.

Methods to Educate Beneficiaries:

- **Provide a Copy of the Trust**: One of the most straightforward ways to ensure your beneficiaries understand the terms of your trust is to give them a copy of the document. They should be able to read the trust and refer to it as needed. If you're uncomfortable giving them a copy of the full document, at least provide them with a summary of the main provisions.

- **Have a Discussion**: Schedule a meeting with your beneficiaries to explain the key points of the trust. This can be a one-on-one meeting or a family meeting, depending on the complexity of your estate. The purpose is to walk them through the trust and answer any questions they may have. Be sure to explain the following:
    - **Who the trustee is** and what their responsibilities entail.
    - **How assets will be distributed** and any specific instructions for special assets or beneficiaries.
    - **How to manage any family businesses**, if applicable.
    - **Who will care for minor children or dependents**, if this is part of your estate plan.
    - **Any instructions for managing digital assets**, including social media accounts and cryptocurrencies.
- **Use a Professional**: If the trust is complex or you anticipate that your beneficiaries may have difficulty understanding the legal jargon, you may want to hire an **estate planning attorney** or financial advisor to explain the terms of the trust. A professional can provide additional clarity and address any legal questions your beneficiaries may have.

4. Timing of Communication

Timing is an important factor when educating your beneficiaries. You should not wait until after your death to have these conversations, as it can create unnecessary confusion and stress. Ideally, you should inform your beneficiaries while you are still alive and able to explain things clearly. Early communication allows your loved ones to ask questions, express concerns, and better understand your estate plan.

When to Communicate:

- **Before You Create the Trust**: If you have a significant family business, special instructions, or complex assets, it's helpful to begin the conversation before you finalize the trust. This gives your beneficiaries time to ask questions, provide input, and ensure that their needs are addressed.

- **After the Trust is Created**: Once the trust is finalized, but before your passing, hold a meeting with the beneficiaries to explain the terms. This ensures that everyone is on the same page and that there are no surprises.
- **During Major Life Changes**: If your family dynamic changes (e.g., the birth of children, divorce, remarriage), it's important to revisit the conversation to ensure that the terms of your trust still reflect your current wishes.

Making Sure Your Loved Ones Understand Your Wishes

It's one thing to explain the terms of the trust to your beneficiaries, but ensuring they **understand your wishes** is another critical aspect of the process. You want to make sure that your intentions are clear and that your loved ones are equipped to carry out your wishes properly. Here's how you can ensure they fully comprehend your estate plan:

1. Clarify Your Intentions

The language used in the trust document itself should be **clear and unambiguous** to avoid confusion later. However, communication with your beneficiaries is just as important. Even if the trust document is clear, explaining your reasoning and desires behind specific decisions can help them better understand the big picture.

Steps to Clarify Your Intentions:

- **Explain the Why**: It's helpful to explain why you've made certain decisions. For example, if you're leaving a business to one child but not the other, you should clarify why this decision was made. The child who is left out may be confused or hurt without an explanation.
- **Discuss Specifics**: Address any **special assets** or considerations. If you're leaving family heirlooms, artwork, or collectibles, explain their significance and why you've chosen certain beneficiaries for these items.
- **Address Complex Situations**: If your estate plan involves complex situations, such as a **special needs child** or a **family business**, provide your beneficiaries with the context behind these decisions.

2. Encourage Beneficiaries to Ask Questions

Encourage open dialogue and questions from your beneficiaries. Sometimes, beneficiaries may feel uncomfortable asking questions or may not fully understand certain aspects of the trust. By fostering an environment where questions are welcome, you ensure that everyone is on the same page and can address any concerns before the trust is executed.

How to Encourage Questions:

- **Be Approachable**: Let your beneficiaries know that you're open to discussing the trust and any concerns they might have.
- **Provide Written Materials**: After the conversation, provide them with written summaries or guides that outline the trust's provisions. This gives them something to refer to and reduces the chance of confusion later.
- **Set a Follow-Up Meeting**: If your beneficiaries have additional questions after the initial discussion, set a follow-up meeting to address them. It's better to answer questions in advance than to deal with confusion after your passing.

3. Use Technology to Your Advantage

In today's digital age, technology can make it easier to manage and share estate planning information. You can use online tools to organize your trust, provide beneficiaries with access to important documents, and ensure transparency.

How to Use Technology:

- **Create a Digital Estate Plan**: You can create a digital version of your estate plan and store it in a secure location (such as a password-protected cloud storage service). Share the login credentials with your beneficiaries and trusted family members to ensure they can easily access the information.
- **Record Video or Audio Messages**: Sometimes, a personal message can help beneficiaries understand your wishes better. You can record a video or audio message explaining your decisions and the reasoning behind them. This personal touch can help reinforce your intentions.

How to Handle Beneficiaries Who Are Not Ready for Inheritance

There may be situations where a beneficiary, despite being legally entitled to inherit assets, is not prepared to manage the wealth they are set to receive. This could apply to children who are too young to understand the value of money, adults who have demonstrated financial irresponsibility, or individuals who lack the experience needed to manage a significant inheritance. In these cases, special provisions must be put in place to prevent the inheritance from being misused or squandered.

1. The Importance of Timing When Distributing Inheritance

One of the most effective ways to handle beneficiaries who are not ready for inheritance is to set **age-based or time-based distribution schedules**. Instead of providing a lump sum to a young or financially inexperienced person, you can specify that assets are distributed gradually over time, or when the beneficiary reaches a certain age or milestone.

Types of Distribution Schedules:

- **Age-Based Distribution**: You can set specific ages at which the beneficiary receives certain portions of their inheritance. For example, you might specify that the beneficiary will receive one-third of their inheritance at age 25, another third at age 30, and the remainder at age 35.
- **Milestone-Based Distribution**: You can link distributions to specific milestones that reflect the beneficiary's maturity or achievements, such as graduating from college, starting a career, or getting married. This ensures that the beneficiary is more likely to be responsible and prepared to handle the funds at the time of distribution.

These provisions help ensure that the inheritance is provided when the beneficiary has reached a level of maturity or responsibility to manage the assets effectively. By spreading out the distributions, you can reduce the risk of an heir squandering their inheritance on poor financial decisions.

2. Setting Up a Trust with Discretionary Distributions

Another option is to establish a **discretionary trust** for the beneficiary. In this scenario, the **trustee** is given the authority to distribute funds to the beneficiary as needed, rather than automatically releasing funds on a specific date. The trustee has the flexibility to withhold distributions until the beneficiary demonstrates financial maturity or reaches a certain level of responsibility.

This approach can be beneficial when:

- The beneficiary is young or not yet financially responsible.
- The beneficiary has shown a history of poor financial decisions (e.g., overspending, addiction issues, etc.).
- The beneficiary is capable of handling smaller, more controlled amounts of money rather than a lump sum.

How Discretionary Trusts Work:

- The **trustee** is responsible for determining when and how much money to give the beneficiary.
- The trust could specify guidelines, such as providing funds for specific purposes (e.g., education, medical expenses, or buying a home) to ensure the money is used responsibly.

Discretionary trusts give the trustee the flexibility to act in the best interest of the beneficiary while preventing them from receiving a large sum of money before they are ready.

3. Including Spendthrift Provisions in Your Trust

A **spendthrift trust** is a trust designed to protect the beneficiary from their own financial mistakes. This type of trust includes a provision that **restricts the beneficiary's ability to access large sums of money all at once**. Spendthrift provisions help safeguard the inheritance from being spent irresponsibly, mismanaged, or seized by creditors.

Spendthrift provisions are particularly helpful in cases where:

- The beneficiary has a history of **addiction** (e.g., gambling or substance abuse) that might lead to poor decision-making.
- The beneficiary lacks the **skills or knowledge** to manage large sums of money effectively.
- The beneficiary is at risk of being taken advantage of by others.

In a spendthrift trust, the trustee controls the distributions, and they are made based on the beneficiary's needs, rather than allowing the beneficiary to withdraw a lump sum. This provides both **protection for the beneficiary** and ensures that the funds are used for their benefit over the long term.

How to Protect Vulnerable Beneficiaries (Children, Disabled, etc.)

Certain beneficiaries, such as children or individuals with special needs, require additional protection in your estate plan to ensure they are provided for without jeopardizing their eligibility for government benefits or leaving them vulnerable to exploitation. There are several tools available that help protect these vulnerable beneficiaries, ensuring they can access the support they need while preventing mismanagement of funds.

1. Setting Up a Special Needs Trust

A **special needs trust** is designed to benefit a person with disabilities or special needs while **preserving their eligibility for government assistance**. In many cases, receiving a large inheritance can disqualify a disabled person from receiving government benefits such as Medicaid, Supplemental Security Income (SSI), or other public assistance programs.

A special needs trust allows you to leave money to a disabled beneficiary without impacting their ability to receive these critical benefits. The trust ensures that the funds are used for their supplemental needs, such as medical care, education, or personal care, without affecting their eligibility for public assistance.

Key Features of a Special Needs Trust:

- **Funds are not counted as income**: Because the trust funds are not directly given to the beneficiary, they are not counted as income for purposes of determining eligibility for government benefits.
- **Trustee control**: The trustee controls how the funds are distributed, ensuring the money is used for the beneficiary's benefit but not impacting their benefits.
- **Legal protection**: A special needs trust provides legal protection for the beneficiary, ensuring they are not taken advantage of by others seeking to exploit their inheritance.

2. Guardianship for Minor Children

When you pass away and leave minor children behind, you need to designate a **guardian** to care for them. Without a guardian in place, the court will decide who will care for your children, which may not align with your wishes. Naming a guardian in your trust or will ensures that your children are cared for by someone you trust and who shares your values.

How to Set Up Guardianship:

- **Choose the Right Guardian**: When choosing a guardian for your children, think carefully about their **age, maturity**, and ability to provide for your children's emotional, financial, and physical needs. It's also important to consider the guardian's relationship with your children and whether they can provide a stable environment.
- **Consider Alternatives**: It may be wise to name **alternate guardians** in case the first choice is unable or unwilling to take on the responsibility. This ensures that your children are never left without a caregiver.

3. Educational Provisions for Minor Beneficiaries

In addition to appointing a guardian, you may also want to include provisions in your trust for the **education of minor children**. If your children are young, you might want to specify how your trust should be used for their schooling and future education expenses.

Some ways to fund your children's education include:

- **Designating Funds for College**: You can create a fund within the trust specifically for **higher education expenses**, ensuring that your children can attend college or university without worrying about funding.
- **Directing Use of Funds**: You can include instructions in the trust specifying that the money should be used for particular educational purposes, such as tuition, books, or extracurricular activities.

How to Protect Vulnerable Beneficiaries from External Threats

In some cases, vulnerable beneficiaries may face threats from external sources, such as creditors, lawsuits, or predatory individuals. For example, a beneficiary with **poor money management skills** could be easily influenced by others to misappropriate funds. Similarly, a person who is financially vulnerable might have their inheritance seized in the event of a lawsuit or other financial hardship.

Protective Strategies for Vulnerable Beneficiaries:

- **Spendthrift Provisions**: As previously mentioned, spendthrift trusts provide a protective mechanism by preventing beneficiaries from accessing large sums of money directly. This ensures that the beneficiary's inheritance is protected from creditors and others who may attempt to seize it.
- **Incorporating Protections in the Trust**: You can include provisions that specifically limit the ability of creditors or third parties to access the funds in the trust. This can prevent a beneficiary from being forced to give up their inheritance in the event of a legal claim or financial hardship.

Chapter 14: Final Thoughts and Next Steps

Reviewing Your Estate Plan Regularly

Just as you would regularly review and update other important documents—like insurance policies, financial plans, or health care directives—your estate plan requires the same level of attention. An up-to-date estate plan helps you avoid complications, ensure that your beneficiaries are taken care of, and reduce the potential for legal disputes. Regularly reviewing your estate plan also ensures that it accurately reflects changes in the law, your family's circumstances, and your financial situation.

Why Regular Reviews Matter

The primary reason for reviewing your estate plan regularly is that **life changes**. As your life evolves, so too should your estate planning documents. By regularly checking your estate plan, you ensure that your assets are distributed as you intend, that your beneficiaries are properly designated, and that your trust continues to meet your goals.

Some reasons why you should review your estate plan periodically include:

- **Change in family dynamics**: Marriage, divorce, children, grandchildren, and other family changes may alter how you want your estate distributed.
- **Change in financial circumstances**: Significant changes in your wealth or the assets you own may require adjustments to your plan, such as adding new assets to your trust.
- **Changes in tax laws**: Estate and gift tax laws may change, which could impact the way you plan for the transfer of wealth.
- **Changes in the law**: In addition to tax law changes, other legal considerations—such as state-specific regulations—may require that your trust be modified to comply with the current laws.

When to Review Your Estate Plan

It is recommended that you review your estate plan at least once every **three to five years**. However, some major life events or changes might necessitate more frequent reviews. Here are several life events that should prompt an immediate review of your estate plan:

1. **Marriage or Divorce**: If you marry, you may want to update your estate plan to include your spouse as a beneficiary or modify the distribution of assets. Conversely, a divorce requires you to change the beneficiaries and possibly even the named trustee.
2. **Birth or Adoption of a Child**: The arrival of a new child or the adoption of a child should be reflected in your estate plan. You will need to update your trust to include the child as a beneficiary and designate guardians for them if they are minors.
3. **Death of a Beneficiary or Trustee**: If someone named in your trust passes away, whether it's a beneficiary, trustee, or anyone who has a role in your estate plan, you will need to update the plan to reflect these changes.
4. **Changes in Financial Situation**: Significant financial changes, such as an inheritance, a large raise, selling a business, or purchasing real estate, should trigger a review. You may want to revise your trust to reflect new assets or modify how your assets are divided among beneficiaries.
5. **Changes in Health**: If you or a family member experience changes in health, such as becoming incapacitated or developing a serious illness, it may be necessary to update healthcare directives or powers of attorney.
6. **Legal or Tax Changes**: Keep an eye on any changes to estate, inheritance, and gift tax laws that may impact your estate plan. If there are significant changes, you should review and possibly adjust your strategy for minimizing taxes.

How to Conduct a Review

When reviewing your estate plan, focus on the following key components:

1. **Review the Trust**: Ensure that the trust document is still aligned with your current wishes. Verify that your trustee, beneficiaries, and distribution instructions are accurate and updated.

2. **Review Beneficiary Designations**: Double-check the beneficiaries listed on life insurance policies, retirement accounts, and other assets outside of the trust. These designations take precedence over your trust instructions, so they must be kept up to date.
3. **Review Powers of Attorney and Healthcare Directives**: Make sure the powers of attorney and healthcare directives are still valid and reflect your current preferences. If you've named someone as your agent, ensure that they are still able and willing to act in your best interest.
4. **Update Assets**: If you've acquired new assets, added or sold property, or experienced changes in asset values, make sure these are properly accounted for in your trust.
5. **Consult an Estate Planning Attorney**: While you can review your plan yourself, it's a good idea to consult with an estate planning attorney to ensure that everything is in order and legally compliant.

How to Keep Your Trust Up-to-Date with Life Changes

In addition to regular reviews, it's essential to ensure that your trust reflects any significant changes in your life. The goal is to ensure that the trust remains relevant and effective in carrying out your wishes, even as your personal, financial, or familial circumstances change.

Here are some practical steps you can take to keep your trust updated:

1. Adjusting for Family Changes

Your family is likely to be the primary beneficiary of your estate, so changes in family dynamics should be closely mirrored in your trust.

- **Adding New Family Members**: When you have a child or grandchild, update the trust to include them as beneficiaries. You'll also want to appoint a guardian for minor children and outline provisions for their care and inheritance.
- **Divorce**: Divorce can dramatically change your estate planning needs. After a divorce, you'll want to ensure that your ex-spouse is removed from your trust and will not inherit any of your assets unless you specifically choose to leave them something. Similarly, if you've remarried, you might want to update the trust to include your new spouse.
- **Death of Family Members**: The death of a loved one requires you to update the trust to reflect that person's absence. You may need to appoint a new trustee or beneficiary, or adjust your distribution plan.
- **Estrangement**: If you become estranged from a family member, you may want to remove them from your trust. Keeping someone in your estate plan against your wishes can create unnecessary complications.

2. Adjusting for Financial Changes

Your financial situation can change over time, and your estate plan should reflect those changes. Whether you acquire significant new assets, like property or investments, or experience a reduction in your wealth, adjusting your trust ensures that your estate plan stays relevant.

- **Adding or Selling Assets**: Whenever you buy or sell assets, remember to update your trust. For example, if you sell a house, you need to remove it from the trust and if you purchase new property, you'll need to transfer it into the trust.
- **Significant Income or Expenditures**: If you come into a large sum of money, such as through an inheritance or the sale of a business, you may want to review your distribution plan. You might decide to allocate a larger portion to charity or create separate trusts for family members based on their needs.

3. Updating Trustees and Executors

You may need to change your trustee or executor over time, especially if they can no longer serve due to personal reasons, illness, or death. The trustee plays an important role in administering your trust, so it's crucial to ensure that the person in charge is trustworthy and capable of carrying out your wishes.

- **Change in Trustee**: If your current trustee is unable or unwilling to serve, update the trust to reflect a new trustee. You can name a family member, a trusted friend, or a professional fiduciary.
- **Naming Successor Trustees**: It's essential to name one or more successor trustees in case the primary trustee becomes incapacitated or unavailable. These individuals should be named in the trust and should be aware of their duties and responsibilities.

4. Adjusting for Changes in Tax Law

Tax laws, both at the state and federal level, are subject to change. These changes could impact your estate's tax liabilities or the way your trust should be structured. Estate taxes, gift taxes, and generation-skipping taxes can all change, so it's important to consult with a tax professional or estate planning attorney to determine if your trust needs adjustments.

For example, if the federal estate tax exemption increases or decreases, you may need to change your estate plan to take advantage of the new thresholds. Similarly, changes in state estate taxes may require you to restructure your assets or beneficiaries.

What Happens If You Don't Review and Update Your Trust Regularly

Neglecting to review and update your trust can lead to serious consequences. If your trust is outdated or doesn't reflect your current wishes, the people you want to inherit your estate might not receive what you intended, or certain assets might be left out of the plan entirely. Additionally, failing to update your trust could result in **tax liabilities** or **legal issues** for your beneficiaries.

Consequences of Not Reviewing Your Trust Regularly:

- **Unintended Beneficiaries**: If your family structure changes and you don't update your trust, someone you don't want to benefit from your estate could inherit assets.
- **Legal Conflicts**: An outdated trust can lead to family disputes and legal battles over your estate. Beneficiaries may contest the trust, which can delay the distribution of assets and increase costs.
- **Probate**: If assets are not properly funded into the trust or the trust is invalidated due to changes in the law, your estate may be subject to probate, causing delays and expenses.

Planning for the Unexpected: What to Do After Major Life Events

No matter how much we plan, life is inherently unpredictable. Major life events can change everything, including your family structure, your financial situation, and your goals. Estate planning is not a one-time task but a dynamic process that requires regular updates to reflect your changing circumstances. The key is to stay flexible and prepared for the unexpected by ensuring that your living trust reflects your current reality.

1. Life Events That Can Impact Your Estate Plan

There are several life events that can trigger the need to review and revise your living trust. These include:

- **Marriage**: When you get married, your estate plan may need to be updated to include your spouse as a beneficiary or to adjust the distribution of assets. It is also important to consider whether the property you already own needs to be transferred into joint ownership or into the name of the trust.
- **Divorce**: Divorce is one of the most significant events that requires updating your estate plan. You may want to remove your ex-spouse from your trust, change beneficiaries, or appoint a new executor. You may also need to update **beneficiary designations** on accounts such as life insurance policies, retirement funds, and bank accounts to ensure that your former spouse is no longer the beneficiary.
- **The Birth or Adoption of Children**: When you have children, your estate plan should be updated to include them as beneficiaries. If they are minors, it's especially important to designate a **guardian** in your trust to ensure their care and protection in the event of your passing.
- **Death of a Loved One**: If a beneficiary, spouse, or trustee dies, your trust must be updated to reflect this change. If your trustee or executor passes away, you will need to appoint a new one. Similarly, if a beneficiary is no longer alive, you must adjust the distribution of

your estate.

- **Acquiring New Assets**: Major financial changes, such as the acquisition of property, investments, or a business, require updates to your trust. You will need to ensure that these assets are properly titled in the name of the trust and allocated to the right beneficiaries.
- **Incapacity**: If you become unable to manage your financial affairs due to illness or incapacity, your estate plan must provide a clear mechanism for how your assets will be handled. Having a **power of attorney** and an **incapacity plan** in place ensures that someone you trust can step in and manage your affairs in a way that aligns with your wishes.

2. Updating Your Trust After Major Life Events

When any of the above events occur, it's important to update your trust promptly. Failure to do so can lead to complications, including:

- **Legal confusion** over who is entitled to your assets.
- **Unintended beneficiaries** receiving assets that you did not intend for them.
- **Increased tax liabilities** due to outdated asset distributions.

How to Update Your Trust After Life Events:

- **Marriage**: After marriage, ensure that your spouse is named as a primary beneficiary in your trust, and update your property holdings to include the spouse as a co-owner or joint tenant. Consider whether you want to create a **joint trust** with your spouse to simplify the distribution of assets upon both of your deaths.
- **Divorce**: After divorce, update your trust to remove your former spouse from any provisions or assets that you no longer wish to share with them. You may also need to revise guardianship provisions if you had previously named your ex-spouse as the guardian of your children.
- **Children**: If you have a child or adopt one, make sure they are named

as a beneficiary in your trust. If the child is a minor, designate a guardian and specify how funds should be managed on their behalf until they reach a certain age.

- **Death of a Beneficiary**: When a beneficiary passes away, you will need to amend your trust to redistribute their portion of the estate. If you had a contingent beneficiary named, the assets will pass to them. Otherwise, the assets may go to a different family member or charity based on your instructions.
- **Incapacity**: Ensure that your trust includes provisions for managing your assets in case you become incapacitated. Appoint someone as a **successor trustee** and provide instructions for how they should manage the trust during your incapacity.

By ensuring that your trust is updated after each major life event, you ensure that your estate plan continues to reflect your current wishes and life circumstances.

Why Your Living Trust Is More Than Just a Document: It's Your Legacy

A living trust is often seen as a tool to **avoid probate**, minimize taxes, and manage asset distribution. However, it serves a much deeper purpose. Your living trust is more than just a document—it is a **reflection of your legacy**. It is your way of ensuring that your life's work, your assets, and your values are passed down to future generations in a way that aligns with your wishes.

1. The Living Trust as a Reflection of Your Values

Beyond the legalities of asset distribution, a living trust allows you to **express your values** and pass them on. Through the trust, you can ensure that:

- Your **philanthropic interests** are preserved. For example, you may want to leave a portion of your estate to a charity, foundation, or cause that you care about.
- Your **business legacy** is maintained. If you own a family business, you can ensure that it remains operational and thrives in the hands of the next generation.
- Your **family values** are upheld. A trust can provide for the education of your children, ensure the care of loved ones with special needs, or designate a guardian for minor children. These provisions reflect your priorities and commitment to your family's well-being.

A well-designed trust helps you leave a legacy that goes beyond money. It ensures that your **ethical principles**, **family traditions**, and **philanthropic efforts** are passed down and honored.

2. The Trust's Role in Preserving Your Family's Future

A living trust plays a crucial role in securing your family's financial future. It provides stability and peace of mind for your loved ones, knowing that the wealth you've accumulated will be passed on according to your wishes. This is particularly important in the event of unexpected life changes or death, where your family may otherwise struggle with probate proceedings, uncertainty about your intentions, or family conflicts.

- **Avoiding Probate**: Without a living trust, your family may face a lengthy and expensive probate process. The trust helps your estate bypass this process, allowing your heirs to receive their inheritance more quickly and efficiently.
- **Reducing Family Conflict**: A clear and comprehensive trust can prevent disputes among family members. By specifying how assets will be distributed, you can reduce the chances of arguments or misunderstandings among beneficiaries.
- **Protecting Beneficiaries**: For beneficiaries who are minors or who have special needs, a living trust can ensure that their inheritance is managed properly. You can designate trustees to handle the funds on their behalf and ensure that they are used for the intended purpose, such as education or healthcare.

3. The Trust's Role in Minimizing Tax Liabilities

A living trust allows you to pass assets to your beneficiaries with minimal tax liabilities. While a trust is not a way to entirely avoid estate taxes, it can provide strategies to reduce your estate's taxable value. This is particularly important for larger estates, where estate taxes could significantly reduce the amount your beneficiaries receive.

Through proper planning, you can structure your trust in a way that minimizes tax burdens, such as by making use of exemptions, charitable donations, and other strategies to reduce taxable assets.

Conclusion

Estate planning is about more than just making sure your assets are passed down—it's about creating a legacy that lasts. A well-crafted estate plan, particularly a **living trust**, ensures that your family and loved ones are provided for according to your wishes, without the complications and delays that can arise from probate or legal disputes. As you reflect on the steps needed to build a comprehensive estate plan, remember that this process is one of the most profound gifts you can give to your family.

The Benefits of Planning Ahead for Your Family

The benefits of creating an estate plan are profound, particularly when you plan ahead. Taking the time to develop a thoughtful estate plan will not only benefit you during your lifetime, but it will also protect your family and future generations.

1. Financial Security for Your Loved Ones

By creating a living trust and clearly outlining your estate plan, you ensure that your family members receive their inheritance with minimal hassle and delay. One of the primary advantages of a living trust is that it allows your assets to bypass the lengthy and costly probate process. This means your beneficiaries will have access to the funds they need, when they need them, rather than being tied up in court for months or even years.

Additionally, a well-structured estate plan can minimize tax liabilities for your beneficiaries, ensuring that they don't lose a significant portion of their inheritance to estate or inheritance taxes.

2. Avoiding Family Conflict

Money can often cause family disputes, particularly when there is ambiguity or a lack of communication. Without a clear estate plan, your family may not understand your wishes, leading to confusion and potential conflict. This is especially true when there are multiple heirs or complex assets involved.

By proactively discussing your estate plan with your family and naming beneficiaries and trustees in your trust, you can prevent misunderstandings. A well-executed estate plan ensures that there is no room for dispute, as your wishes are documented and legally binding.

3. Protecting Vulnerable Family Members

Some family members may need special consideration in your estate plan, such as children, elderly parents, or loved ones with disabilities. A living trust allows you to set aside provisions to ensure that they are properly cared for and that their inheritance is protected.

For example, a **special needs trust** can provide for a child with disabilities without jeopardizing their eligibility for government assistance. Similarly, by naming a guardian in your trust, you ensure that minor children are cared for by someone you trust. Additionally, setting up a spendthrift trust can protect vulnerable beneficiaries from squandering their inheritance.

4. Preserving Your Business Legacy

If you own a family business, planning for its future is a vital part of your estate planning process. A well-thought-out **business succession plan** ensures that your business remains in good hands, whether it's passed on to a family member or sold to a trusted partner. Without such a plan, the future of the business could be jeopardized, and conflicts may arise among heirs or employees.

By clearly outlining the transfer of ownership and management in your trust, you can preserve your business legacy and ensure its continued success.

The Peace of Mind You Get from a Well-Executed Estate Plan

One of the greatest benefits of creating a living trust and having a comprehensive estate plan is the peace of mind it provides. Knowing that your family will be taken care of, your wishes will be honored, and your assets will be properly distributed brings comfort.

1. Control Over Your Assets and Legacy

A living trust gives you control over how your assets are distributed after your death. You can decide who receives what, when they receive it, and under what conditions. This level of control ensures that your estate plan aligns with your values and that your loved ones receive the benefit of your thoughtful planning.

Additionally, a well-executed estate plan can include provisions for charitable giving, ensuring that your legacy reflects your commitment to causes you care about.

2. Reducing the Burden on Your Family

Without a plan in place, your family may face significant burdens in managing your estate after you're gone. This can include the emotional stress of navigating probate, the financial stress of paying estate taxes, and the logistical stress of handling unfinished business. With a living trust, your family won't have to worry about managing your affairs after your death—they can focus on grieving and honoring your memory, rather than handling the legal and financial complexities of your estate.

3. Ensuring a Smooth Transition

Whether it's the transfer of assets, the operation of a family business, or the care of minor children, a well-executed estate plan ensures that everything transitions smoothly. The clarity and certainty that come with having a living trust in place minimize the potential for delays, disputes, or confusion. With a clear plan in place, your family can move forward with confidence, knowing that your wishes are being honored.

Your Next Steps in Protecting Your Family's Future

Now that you understand the importance of creating a living trust and the benefits it brings, it's time to take action. The following steps will help guide you through the process of setting up an estate plan that works for you and your loved ones.

1. Take Inventory of Your Assets

The first step in creating your estate plan is to take an inventory of all the assets you own. This includes real estate, bank accounts, retirement accounts, business interests, life insurance policies, personal property, and digital assets (e.g., social media accounts, cryptocurrencies, online businesses). Having a complete list of assets will allow you to determine what needs to be transferred into your trust and how you want them distributed.

2. Decide Who Will Be Your Trustee and Beneficiaries

Selecting a trustee and beneficiaries is a critical part of the process. Your trustee is responsible for managing the trust and ensuring that your assets are distributed according to your wishes. Choose someone trustworthy, organized, and capable of managing financial and legal matters. Additionally, decide who will be your beneficiaries and how you want your assets distributed among them.

If you have minor children or other vulnerable beneficiaries, make sure to name a **guardian** for them in your trust and consider setting up special provisions to protect their inheritance.

3. Consult with an Estate Planning Professional

While you can create a trust on your own with templates or online tools, working with an estate planning attorney ensures that your trust is properly drafted, legally sound, and compliant with state laws. An attorney can help you navigate complex issues, such as tax planning, business succession, and digital assets, and will ensure that your estate plan addresses your unique circumstances.

4. Fund Your Trust

Once your trust is created, you need to **fund it** by transferring ownership of your assets into the name of the trust. This is a critical step in the process—without funding your trust, your assets will not be protected from probate. Make sure to transfer real estate, bank accounts, investment accounts, and other valuable assets into the trust.

5. Review Your Trust Regularly

Once your trust is set up and funded, it's important to review it periodically to ensure that it continues to meet your needs. Life changes—such as marriage, divorce, the birth of children, or changes in financial circumstances—may require you to update your trust. Schedule regular reviews (at least once every three to five years) to ensure that your estate plan is up to date.

6. Communicate Your Plan to Your Family

Lastly, ensure that your family is aware of your estate plan. While it's not necessary to share every detail, it's important to let your trustee and beneficiaries know that the trust exists, where it is stored, and what they need to do once you are gone. Open communication about your intentions will help avoid confusion or disputes later on.

Dear Reader,

Thank you for taking the time to explore **The Ultimate Living Trust & Estate Planning Blueprint**. I'm truly honored that you've chosen this book to guide you through the process of protecting your assets, safeguarding your family's future, and creating a lasting legacy.

By investing in your estate planning, you're taking an essential step to ensure that your wishes are respected, your loved ones are cared for, and your legacy is preserved for generations to come. I hope the strategies and insights shared in this book empower you to take control of your future with confidence and clarity.

If you found the book helpful and insightful, I'd be incredibly grateful if you could take a moment to leave a sincere review. Your feedback not only helps others who are considering this important step in their own estate planning but also allows me to continue providing valuable, actionable content to those who need it most.

Thank you again for trusting this book with your estate planning journey. Wishing you all the best in creating a secure, prosperous future for yourself and your loved ones.

With gratitude,

Ernest Garrett

www.ingramcontent.com/pod-product-compliance
Lightning Source LLC
LaVergne TN
LVHW052320200926
848481LV00002B/613